CSLI
Lecture Notes
Number 2

EMOTION
AND FOCUS

by

Helen Fay Nissenbaum

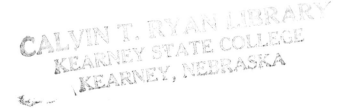

Published by

CSLI   CENTER FOR THE STUDY
        OF LANGUAGE
        AND INFORMATION

Ventura Hall • Stanford University • Stanford, CA 94305

Contents

Introduction

I approach this study of emotion through one of its definitive features: its object directedness. My aim is to discover the conception of emotion that is couched in a commonsense view of the world and is reflected in ordinary discourse on emotion. This conception must make sense of the fact that one loves *someone*, dreads *something*, is angry over *something*. A theory of emotion's object directedness invariably presupposes a particular conception of emotion; a theory of emotion frequently adopts a particular view on object directedness. Theories of both these types are in need of revision at the level of their most basic assumptions.

After examining several prominent views on object directedness, including those of Hume, Kenny, and J. R. S. Wilson, I conclude that the notion is no longer a viable one. I propose a reconceptualization of the phenomena that it is seen to cover. The result is a breakdown of object directedness into a number of independent conceptual units that I call "aspects of emotional episodes." I reject the picture of emotion traditionally forwarded in academic writings, offering another in its place, one that preserves the complexity and variation suggested in the common conception of emotion.

I conclude by bringing together the revised picture of emotion and the alternative conception of object directedness. The two parts of my theory merge harmoniously. The revised picture of emotion has all the ingredients needed to construct an analysis of a significant aspect of its directedness: relation to a focus.

Part One is devoted to an examination of the issue of object directedness. I begin in Chapter 1 by enumerating several of the intuitions that have grounded the notion in the first place. Each of these intuitions gives rise to a possible condition on object directedness, something that must be true about an emotion for it to have an object. One is the idea that in an object-directed emotion the emotion is related to an item in the world; another, that object directedness arises out of a feature of the emotional state alone; and a third, that the object contains explanatory information. In Chapter 2, I discuss critically seven views on object directedness, covering a wide range of positions and showing how some of the intuitions are incorporated into them. Hume, who is said to have originated the idea, and Wilson analyze the *relation* of emotion to object; Rorty and Solomon discuss the intentionality of emotion; and Kenny and Thalberg derive the notion of object directedness from a feature of linguistic descriptions of emotions. I argue that the philosophical literature no longer sustains a viable notion of object directedness. The influences that have molded it are too diverse, resulting in a concept that is so overloaded that even sensible disagreement is precluded. We no longer know *what* the objects of emotion are nor what *makes* them the objects of emotion.

In Chapter 3, I conclude Part One with a suggestion for reconceptualizing the diverse phenomena that have previously been identified under the one notion: "object directedness." I replace the emotion-object pair with the complex picture of an emotional episode. Some of the phenomena previously conceived to be objects of emotions now appear in the guise of "aspects of emotional episodes." In the rest of the book, I limit attention to one of these aspects only, one that I call the emotion's focus. My ultimate goal is to produce an analysis of the relation of emotion to focus. To achieve this, I turn to the question of the nature of emotion.

In Part Two, I turn my attention to the nature of emotion. I uncover two theses that are implicit in almost all academic works on emotion and claim that for a significant class of emotions, including love, envy, fear, and resentment, the theses are not valid. In Chapter 4, I argue that these emotions are nonoccurrent, challenging the validity of the second thesis. My argument for the relationality of certain emotions, the challenge to the first thesis, comes only in Chapter 7. In Chapter 5, I offer an analysis of nonoccurrent, relational emotions, suggesting that an emotional relation is an emergent feature of a sequence of events. The relation is dispositional in that it suggests constraints on the events that it covers. I limit the scope of my theorizing to a class of emotions that I call "active emotions." In Chapter 6, I speculate on the substantial nature of emotional relations. The potential constituents of emotional relations are events in which the subject of the emotion is thinking, acting, or feeling.

The rejoining of the theory of emotion's object directedness, now a theory of aspects of emotion, and the theory of emotion occurs in Part Three. I show how the new theory of emotion yields an analysis of emotion's focus. I end with a review of new directions for research on emotion that are generated by my theory.

Types and Instances (A Word on Terminology). Notice how the emotion terms are used in the following phrases: "Sylvia's emotion," "explaining an emotion you might…" "…whether a statement explains a phenomenon—in this case, an emotion." These expressions are ambiguous because it is impossible to judge whether the term "emotion" is being used to refer to a *type* or an *instance*. I make a few remarks on this issue to try to forestall confusion.

The term "emotion" is used as a label for an aspect of human being—mind and, possibly, body. This use is exemplified in the sentence "Emotion is what really distinguishes man from automaton." It refers to the "grand" type. When it is used in this way it has no plural form, strongly paralleling the uses of terms like "color" and "action" in the sentences "Color is an important factor in the mating habits of guppies" and "In his book, Kenny makes a study of action."

The term may be used to designate the emotion's type, such as anger, jealousy, loathing, and loving. These are emotions but are types, too. They are subtypes of the grand type "emotion." When it is used to designate type, "emotion" does have a plural form. It is used in this way in "The emotions anger and indignation are difficult to distinguish from each other." Similarly, there are colors—blue, red, and yellow—and actions—walking, giving, and eating.

Finally, there are the instances, which are actual pieces of the world consisting of individuals having emotions at locations. We use expressions like "*X* having an emotion" to refer to instances of emotion and sentences like "Sylvia is jealous of her younger brother" to describe situations in which a subject is having an emotion. These three levels might admit of intervening ones.

The cases I cite above are ambiguous in that they are capable of describing emotions at several possible levels. "Sylvia's emotion" refers either to the *type* of Sylvia's emotion (e.g., jealousy) or to an instance, which in this case is Sylvia's current state. In the second and third expressions, the ambiguity is once again between type and instance. One might be meaning that a phenomenon explains an occurrence of an emotion, an instance, or that it explains its type.

It is often very difficult to prevent the ambiguity in certain expressions. Strangely, a sentence will often make perfectly good sense with both readings. Where it is especially unclear, or especially important that a particular reading is made, I draw attention to its intended meaning.

Acknowledgements

This book, adapted from my Ph.D. Dissertation, was prepared while I was a post-doctoral research affiliate at the Center for the Study of Language and Information. The Center has been an exciting intellectual setting for my work, giving me the rare opportunity to interact with, and learn from, many fine scholars in related disciplines. I have benefitted from this enormously and am indebted both to those whose hard work and vision gave rise to CSLI and to the System Development Foundation for making it come about.

In preparing the text of this work, I gratefully acknowledge the assistance of Dianne Kanerva, Dikran Karagueuzian, and Jamie Marks.

PART ONE

Object Directedness

Chapter 1

The Problem of Object Directedness

"Odd that one can identify a pain as 'missing so and so'."
Iris Murdoch, *The Sea, The Sea.*

Murdoch points to a feature of emotion that few would dispute. Emotions are "odd" because they combine two very different elements of the mental: We feel them as we feel pain, but like thoughts and actions they are directed to or are about things. Philosophers who have theorized about emotion have stressed the importance of their directedness. No theory of emotion is complete if it does not include an account of its object directedness. Hume gives only a brief account of the experience of a passion but goes to great lengths in defining its object.[1] Anthony Kenny claims that object directedness is a definitive feature of emotion. He writes, "Emotions, unlike sensations, are essentially directed to objects... It is not possible to be ashamed without being ashamed of anything in particular."[2] And when one considers even the most straightforward descriptions of emotions, their directedness comes across as plain fact. Consider the following examples:

1. Frank loves Susan.
2. Meryl loathes her boss.
3. Paul regrets having refused to invest in Apple Computers.
4. David is dreading seeing his ex-wife.

---

[1] D. Hume, *A Treatise of Human Nature*, Book II.

[2] A. Kenny, *Action, Emotion and Will*, p. 60.

5. Hannah is angry that she was not invited to the party.
6. Selwyn was delighted with the kitten.
7. Clive was distressed over the financial losses of his business.
8. John fears a nuclear war.
9. Stephen is ashamed of the way he treated the beggar.

Philosophers who have theorized about emotion's object directedness have founded their theories on two presuppositions: (i) All or most emotions are directed, and (ii) single conception of directedness covers all cases of object-directed emotions. This means that analyzing this central feature, common to all cases of directed emotions, is a crucial step in constructing a theory of emotion. Taken at face value, these presuppositions are sound. The cases described in statements 1–9 show the extensive range and variation in the types of emotions that are object directed. This weighs in favor of (i). It is reasonable to identify the objects of the emotions to be the person Frank loves, the person Meryl loathes, the decision Paul regrets, events that angered Hannah and distressed Clive, the possibility John fears, and so forth. This supports the doctrine expressed in (ii), that these cases share a common feature.

It is a central contention of Part One of this work that the doctrine expressed in (ii) is unsound and that the notion of object directedness based upon it is simply not viable. I agree that there is something importantly different between emotion and mere sensation that is reflected in statements 1–9. However, I disagree that a single notion can be brought to bear in identifying these differences. The concept of object directedness covers too many distinct intuitions. If one tries to define a notion that preserves all the intuitions, the notion one arrives at will be incoherent. There are several features, not just one, exemplified in statements 1–9. It is the task of a theory of emotion to disentangle these features. Individual theories of object directedness have tended to focus on one of the features, treating it as .if it applied in all cases. This has resulted in all sorts of internal problems for these theories, and because they do not converge on a single notion, sensible comparison is precluded. This multiplicity of phenomena swept together under a single concept is what I have identified as *the problem of object directedness*. It is a problem that comes of treating a cluster of distinct phenomena as if they were the same. I develop this claim here and in the two chapters following. I show how the problem surfaces when one tries to compare different views on object directedness. I conclude Part One with a suggestion for reconceptualizing the domain.

1. Steps Toward a Conception of Object Directedness

I begin looking at the issue of directedness from the perspective created by the two presuppositions. It is no use looking to the notion of directedness itself for substantial insights into the nature of object-directed emotion because its application to emotion is clearly metaphorical. Its explanatory bearing on emotion becomes evident only when one already has a good idea of what an object-directed emotion is. Therefore, one must turn directly to the cases of object-directed emotions to see what they have in common and use this as a basis for one's analysis.

Consider the steps to be taken toward a theory of object directedness. One begins with a set of cases that are positive cases of object-directed emotions according to an intuitively grounded notion. Statements 1–9 describe a sample of this set. Next, one examines the cases for features they have in common that are critical to their being object directed and sets them down as conditions on object directedness. The conditions say what must be true of an emotion for it to qualify as a case of directed emotion. In the ideal situation, the conditions are necessary and jointly sufficient for object directedness. With the exception of J. R. S. Wilson, those who propose theories make no attempt to meet so strict a requirement. The theory one constructs incorporates and elaborates the conditions judged to be critical. The outcome one aims for is an articulated picture of a typical case of object-directed emotion. Ultimately, one returns to the cases as a source of dialectical testing of one's theory.

According to this picture, theories may differ from each other in at least two ways. They may acknowledge distinct sets of conditions on object directedness or, even if they accept a common set of conditions, they may differ according to the way they elaborate the conditions. The first of the two ways results in a far greater divergence because the conditions effectively delineate the domain of investigation. Because the cases of object directed emotions form such a heterogeneous class, the sets of conditions proposed by distinct theories rarely overlap. In fact, some of the conditions are mutually incompatible. This makes the comparison between distinct theories very difficult, because they differ not only in what they say about object-directed emotions but also in what they take to be the very subject matter under investigation. According to my positive thesis, this reflects the fact that there are actually several distinct notions being offered under the guise of object directedness.

2. Four Conditions on Object Directedness

In this section, I discuss four conditions on object directedness. I select these conditions because they are featured either singly or in some combination in all the theories of object directedness that I have seen, either explicitly adopted or implicit in other theoretical stipulations. I classify the views discussed in Chapter 2 according to the four conditions. The conditions are to be taken independently of one another and not seen as four constituents of *one* possible analysis of object directedness. The conjunction of all four conditions in one theory is precluded by the fact that certain combinations of the conditions are incompatible. This accounts for the fact that certain of the views discussed below are incommensurable and is at the bottom of certain disagreements among them. I say more on this in the next two chapters.

Emotion and Object: A Relation. According to this condition, an emotion is object directed if it is related in a certain way to an item in the world. Perhaps the most straightforward condition on directedness, it seems adequately to capture emotion's directedness in simple cases of loving, hating, despising, and being angry. One's loving is directed if there is someone whom one loves; hatred is directed to a human individual; one is angry at someone or about a certain event. The condition is not complete, however, until one deals with the question of the nature of the relation between an emotion and its object. As I mentioned earlier, one does not learn much from the notion of *directedness* because the notion is used metaphorically only, in making reference to the emotion-object relation.

The relational condition has two possible forms. Most theories that incorporate a relational condition claim that an emotion has an object if there is an item in the world that is related in a certain way to the subject's having an emotion. In statement 1, shown earlier, Susan is the object of Frank's loving if she is related to Frank's emotional state in the appropriate way, that is, if she is related to Frank's experience of love. A simple theory based on this form of the condition is one that requires the object of the emotion to be the cause of the subject's having the emotion. This form of the condition rests on a picture of emotion that I characterize in Chapter 4 with two theses. The relational condition in its other form requires that Frank and Susan be related in the appropriate way in order that Susan be considered the object of Frank's emotion. The statement "Frank loves Susan" describes a relation between Frank and Susan. This implies a relational interpretation of "loving" and is an interpretation that I argue for in Parts Two and Three.

I limit the class of theories that incorporate the relational condition to those that characterize the emotion-object relation as a real relation holding between a person's emotion and an item in the world belonging to one of the ordinary ontological categories that a commonsense metaphysics might permit. In other words, I do not classify as properly relational a condition that explicates object directedness in terms of a merely formal relation.

The nature of the relation imposes limitations on the range of items allowable as the objects of emotions. A theory that incorporates a relationality condition must therefore not only elaborate the nature of the relation but must give a consistent account of the types of items toward which emotions may be directed. The range of ontological categories could include some or all of the following: individuals (animate and inanimate), states of affairs, properties, relations, and events. Besides Frank's loving Susan, other examples of object-directed emotions that appear to satisfy the relational condition are Meryl's loathing her boss and Paul's regretting having refused to invest in Apple Computers. In the first two, the emotion is related to a human individual; in the third, to an event. Of the views discussed in the following chapter, Hume's, Wilson's, and to some extent Arnold's, incorporate the relational condition.[3]

Frequently, the expressions used in an analysis of an emotion's object directedness reflect the nature of the conditions it adopts. In particular, a relational view uses terms like "the emotion-object relation" and "the objects of emotion," claims that the emotion is "directed to an object," and may question of particular instances of an emotion what its object is. Unless one takes a relation as one's basic unit and posits real items as one's relata, these expressions have no literal interpretation.

Object Directedness as Intentionality. Another picture of emotion's directedness, conditions directedness on a feature of the emotional state, or experience, making no reference to an independently existing, concrete relatum. An emotion is object directed insofar as it has the features that mark many other types of mental states intentional, or directed. If it is

---

[3] M. B. Arnold, *Emotion and Personality*; D. Hume, *op.cit.*; J. R. S. Wilson, *Emotion and Object*.

possible to show that an instance of an emotion possesses these features, whatever one judges them to be, one concludes that the emotion is object directed. Directed emotions are therefore special cases of directed mental acts (or states). Kenny and Solomon theorize about emotion's directedness in this way.[4] I refer to this condition as the *intentional state condition*.

Most who adopt the hypothesis that directed emotions are special cases of intentional mental acts draw on the tradition of phenomenology for the key notion of intentionality. Within this tradition, mental acts are distinguished on the grounds of their directedness to objects. Directedness to an object is not taken literally to be relatedness to a concrete item in the world but interpreted as a relation of the mental act to an abstract object. Abstract, intentional objects are different from so-called extensional objects in important ways. Brentano, a precursor of the phenomenological tradition, describes the intentionality of the mental in the following passage:

> Every psychical phenomenon is characterized by what the medieval scholastics called the intentional (or mental) existence of an object, and what we, not quite unambiguously, would call "relation to a content," "object directedness" or "immanent objectivity" ("object" here does not mean reality). Each such phenomenon contains in itself something as an object though not each in the same manner. In imagination something is imagined, in judgement something is accepted or rejected, in love something is loved, in hatred something is hated. In desire something is desired and so forth.[5]

In not restricting the objects of emotion to the everyday fixtures of the world, this condition allows for a greater range of cases of object-directed emotions. In particular, even in cases of emotion in which the object is illusory, one is able to account for its object directedness in terms of this intentional existent. In addition, it offers a way of analyzing directedness where the object is propositional or is future oriented, as in the case of being angry *that* one was not invited to the party, or is dreading a future meeting with one's ex-wife. In taking emotion's object directedness to be similar to the directedness of other attitudes, the condition allows for the possibility of object-directed emotion that is nonveridical, that is, for the emotion to be directed to non actual states of affairs, to individuals who do not exist,

---

[4] A. Kenny, Action, Emotion and Will and R. C. Solomon, *The Passions*.

[5] Excerpt from A.Kenny,*Action, EmotionandWill* quoting fromBrentano's *Psychologie von Empirischen Standpunkt*, Book II, Chapter 1, section 5.

to the future, and to the merely possible. This feature is paralleled in the cases of various types of attitudes, including believes, supposes, hopes, and desires.

A disadvantage of this condition is that it implies a new order of existence, that of the intentional object. Critics frequently point out the obscurity of this step. Indeed, many theories provide no insight whatever into the nature of these objects, failing to specify the structure they may possess. Two possibilities exist, both of which are problematic in their own ways. Intentional objects could be mental entities—ideas, for example—or they could be abstract objects that are independent of a particular thinker, something like Fregean senses.

Before moving to the third condition, I make a few remarks about terminology. As in the case of the relational condition, certain descriptive phrases are appropriate in describing theories that are committed to the intentional-state condition. For example, one talks about the *intentional objects* of emotion, refers to the fact of emotion's *intentionality*, and asserts that an emotion *has* an intentional object, that the objects of emotion are intentional. I associate these expressions with views on object directedness that incorporate the intentional-state condition—with one caveat.

It is common to find "intentionality" used interchangeably with "object directedness." The intentionality of emotion is the same phenomenon as emotion's object directedness. That is, as used in this way, there is no commitment to any particular condition on object directedness. It may turn out that emotion's intentionality is relational, as described in the discussion of the first condition. Accordingly, one might use the term "intentional object" to describe any object toward which an emotion is directed, with no ontological commitments one way or the other.

An *intentional state* is a state that is directed toward an intentional object. This classification is an extremely important one because it is frequently assumed that object directedness is partially or completely specifiable in terms of features of a subject's state. Here, too, there is a theory-laden and a theory-free use of the term. One might limit the use of "intentional state" to describe states directed to abstract intentional objects, or one might apply it to any directed state, no matter what the nature of its object. The idea of an intentional state is especially useful in theorizing about cases of emotions that appear to be directed but for which no concrete object exists. It is believed that the directedness of such emotions is a property of the subject's intentional state alone.

I adopt the following conventions. I reserve the term "intentional object" for the objects posited in theories that incorporate the intentional-state condition. In using the terms "object directedness" and "intentionality of emotion," I imply no automatic theoretical commitment. Any conditions assumed will be independently specified. The term "intentional state" lies somewhere in between. I do not limit its use to descriptions of theories in which the objects are intentional. But I use it in describing theories that presuppose that, by virtue of a systematic occurrence of certain sets of intrinsic features of emotional states, they are intentional states.

I draw attention briefly to a point of contrast between this condition and the relationality condition. In the latter, the unit most relevant to directedness is a relation. Object directednesss of an emotion is conditioned upon the presence or absence of a relation of a certain type, between someone's having an emotion and an item in the world. It could be compared to a naive realist's picture of perception. It is conceivable, according to this condition, that emotion's object directedness be characterized in purely relational terms, that is, without considering the issue of whether an emotional state is an intentional-state. By contrast, the intentional state condition makes the intentional state the unit of interest. Because intentional objects are not ordinary objects of a commonsense world, the only route to these objects is through the intentional state. This has implications for typical problems faced by theories that incorporate one or other of the conditions. The relationality condition makes it difficult to account for the cases in which an emotion appears to be directed but for which no object exists. Conversely, simple relational cases like the one described by "Frank loves Susan" present a challenge to theories that incorporate the intentional-state condition, for it is not obvious how to tie an intentional state to a concrete item. In Chapter 2, I examine how various theorists have attempted to deal with these cases.

The Linguistic Condition. A third alternative is to condition object directedness of emotion upon a feature of descriptions of emotions. A theory of object directedness incorporates what I call a "linguistic condition" if it ties the object directedness of emotion to certain structural features of sentences that describe emotions. According to a theory that incorporates the linguistic condition, one decides the question of an emotion's directedness by seeing whether a description of the emotion satisfies a proposed set of stipulations. It is possible for distinct theories to incorporate a linguistic condition but to disagree on the exact nature of the stipulations that mark object directedness.

It is not easy to see how one might develop a theory that upholds a linguistic condition given the variation in the ways we describe emotions. One sees this even in the limited sample of cases presented earlier in the statements 1–9.[6] However, there are subsets in which the cases resemble one another quite substantially. For example, instances of several types of emotions are described with sentences in which the emotion is designated by a transitive verb, followed by a grammatical object expression. These are similar to sentences with transitive verbs that describe actions. Another subgroup is suggested by cases resembling descriptions of the so-called propositional attitudes. The subjects are angry that, delighted about, or distressed over something. The 'something' is designated by a complex linguistic expression and is frequently called a "proposition."

Frege's writings are largely responsible for initiating a theorizing about the nature of mental acts and psychological states, which is based on features of the way we talk about these states. Sentences like "Hannah is angry that she was not invited to the party" bear so strong a formal resemblance to the sentences that Frege examined directly that it is tempting to try to extend a Fregean analysis to them. One might consider emotion's directedness to involve a subject having a certain attitude to the *thought* expressed by the *that*-clause. Yet one need not uphold Frege's semantic theory to be considered a supporter of the linguistic condition. All it requires is a commitment to the assumption that the structure of sentences describing emotions reflects the structure of the world and, in particular, emotion's object directedness.

A linguistic condition does not automatically preclude either of the previous conditions. It requires only that features of the *descriptions* of emotions are the primary determiners in deciding whether or not an emotion is directed. A theory that incorporates a linguistic condition might also adopt one of the other conditions depending on the details of the linguistic condition it incorporates. One's linguistic condition might limit the permissible sentences describing object-directed emotion to one of the subgroups mentioned above. For example, if transitive emotion verbs in the active voice form the chosen category, the relationality condition is favored. If, on the other hand, sentences like "Mary is afraid that the man following her will harm her" are judged paradigmatic of descriptions of object-directed emotions, the second condition is preferred.

---

[6] See the Appendix for further examples.

Objects Have Explanatory Value.   A fourth condition on object directedness requires that an emotion's object play an explanatory role with respect to the emotion. According to this condition, refusing to invest in a company that would have earned him millions of dollars is the object of Paul's regret because one cites his refusal in explaining Paul's regret. Similarly, to explain Hannah's anger one cites the fact that she was not invited to the party, and the financial loss of his business is explanatorily relevant to Clive's distress. The condition restricts object directedness in the following way: In citing whatever it is that one identifies to be the object of a directed emotion, one *explains* the emotion. Rorty adheres to the explanatory condition in requiring an emotion's object to be the rationale for the emotion.

The explanatory condition is not clearly sufficient for object directedness for consider the following: An event's cause is explanatorily relevant to the event. That is, in explaining an event one frequently cites its cause. An emotion's cause may not be its object. Take, for example, an emotional state induced by a drug: One feels happy, optimistic, and content over one's future because of the cocaine, but this is not the object of one's emotion. I discuss this issue in greater detail in the next chapter.

3. The Problem

We are presented with a dilemma. Each of the four conditions respects a facet of the intuition behind object directedness. Theories that incorporate the conditions preserve the appropriately connected facets of the intuitive notion. I acknowledged that a combination of the conditions is permissible within a theory. However, any theory that would attempt to cover the full intuitive notion and therefore incorporate all four conditions would be incoherent. One faces a dilemma in having to decide between a theory that attempts to respect the full extent of the intuitive underpinning and therefore is incoherent and one that analyzes a more limited notion and therefore fails to give a complete account of all that has come to be associated with emotion's object directedness.

This dilemma can be expressed in different terms. Recall the statements 1–9, descriptions of object-directed emotions as sanctioned by the intuitive conception. Imagine that these are descriptions of a mere sample of a set containing more of the same types of cases. The sample itself reflects the heterogeneity of the entire class. This proves a stumbling block in the way of defining a concept of directedness that covers the class of cases. To succeed with ones definition one looks for principles that cover the distinct cases. I claim that this is impossible. The best one is able to do is to pick out distinct clusters of cases that one recognizes because the members share a notable common feature. There is no obvious, significant feature that is common to the entire class. It is obviously easier to formulate a condition on membership to the individual clusters than to do so for the entire class. One faces the dilemma of deciding between a theory of object directedness that covers only a small cluster of the cases included in the intuitively generated class or being stuck with the apparently impossible task of finding a condition that covers the entire class.

Many theories have implicitly chosen the first option, so that even though they are termed theories of object directedness they are theories of a more limited notion. The limited notion is generated by the smaller cluster of cases for which a unifying principle is identifiable. It is a further thesis of my analysis that one is prevented from a simple merging of all suggested conditions because they are not all mutually compatible. I discuss this assertion more fully in the next and the third chapters. I conclude that the class of object-directed emotions generated by the intuitive notion does not support the possibility of a precisely formulated and interesting principle. The principles, some of which are exemplified in the four conditions, cover clusters of cases and not the entire class.

One might argue that a universal condition could be constructed by disjoining the conditions that cover distinct clusters of cases. This might solve the problem of several merely partial analyses, but it is bound to lead to an artificial notion with no utility in furthering our understanding of emotion. In the discussion of Kenny's view, I compare the utility of a conception of this generality to one described by "plant, or red and cubic, or an insect that travels faster than fifteen miles per hour." The contribution to our understanding of emotion would be far greater if we would consider separately the distinct phenomena that are represented in the individual clusters. I follow up this recommendation in Chapter 3.

Several general conditions on object directedness have emerged in the attempt to give the notion a precise formulation. Each of the conditions, or coherent combinations of the conditions, is satisfied by a cluster of the original class and not by the whole one. This points to the fact that there is no single concept (of a nonartificial nature) that generates the entire class but several distinct concepts. The conditions are not rival conditions in an analysis of a single concept but conditions that select distinct phenomena from the original class. Any attempt to provide an analysis of a concept that covers all the cases sampled in 1–9 is bound to fail. In proposing that the study of object directedness be abandoned, I propose that we cease looking for a single concept underlying the entire heterogeneous class, not that we abandon the study of the several interesting but distinct concepts that the cases exemplify. In pursuing this program, the dialectical testing of the distinct concepts is limited to the cluster of its expected positive instances.

In the next chapter, I consider the evidence in favor of my thesis, that the notion of object directedness is not a viable one, by examining and comparing several unsuccessful attempts to explicate the notion. Some of these take the form of quite detailed theories of emotion's object directedness, while others comprise no more than remarks on the nature of emotions and their objects. I appraise these views in two ways: first, by evaluating their internal structure and, second, by ascertaining the extent to which they succeed in representing the intuitive components of object directedness. I find them lacking in both ways. It is actually a consequence of my thesis that any attempt to provide an analysis of object directedness is doomed to failure unless the domain of inquiry is drastically limited. I use the theories to illustrate my claim that certain combinations of the conditions are impossible. According to the recommendation of the previous paragraph, instead of viewing the theories as competing theories of one phenomenon, they are more accurately regarded as theories of diverse phenomena directed to distinct clusters of test cases.

Chapter 2

Views on Object Directedness

I now describe the views on object directedness put forward in some of the most prominent accounts of emotion. As I have mentioned before, these range in format from well-thought-out and fairly complete theories to one or two remarks expressing the commitment of the theorist in question to some picture or other of emotion's object directedness. I look in some detail at the accounts of David Hume, Anthony Kenny, and J. R. S. Wilson and more cursorily at the views of Amelie Rorty, Robert Solomon, Magda Arnold, and Irving Thalberg.

1. Hume

Hume is recognized as the first philosopher to have drawn attention to the difference between the object of an emotion and its cause or eliciting condition. Hume's views on objects of emotion may be seen as a conceptual first in that they contain the kernel of later proposals and, in addition, spawn many contemporary disputes.[1] Despite this, it is a mistake to see Hume's own explication as an attempt at a full-blown theory of object directedness, because he makes little effort to conjure up a general notion of emotion as directed to an object. He limits his discussion of the notion to its application to a few special cases including pride, humility, love, and hatred.

Hume explicitly adopts the metaphysics laid out in the first book of the *Treatise* for his discussion of the passions and their objects. This cov-

---

[1] My source for Hume's treatment of object directedness of emotion is D. Hume, *Treatise on Human Nature*, Book II ("Of the Passions"), L. A. Selby-Bigge (ed.).

ers his stipulations concerning the components of consciousness, that is impressions and ideas, and the principles governing their succession. The similarity relation and the relation of cause to effect are particularly relevant to his explication of the passions.[2] In looking at all the notions Hume discusses in Book I and uses in Book II, it is perhaps most important to maintain a clear idea of what he makes of the cause-effect relation, since it is in contrast with an emotion's cause that its object acquires certain general characteristics.

This is Hume's picture. A passion, which is a simple and uniform impression of reflexion, is one component of a stereotypic causal sequence. Unlike impressions of sensation, which are direct consequences of sensory input, impressions of reflexion are impressions following, and arising from, ideas. A passion is preceded by an idea that causes it and is followed by an idea that *it* causes. Hume says of the second idea in the sequence that the empassioned soul's "view always fixes" on this idea. I say "stereotypic," since it is not the case that a passion can be sandwiched between just any sequence of ideas. Only ideas of certain types of states of affairs and items in the world elicit emotions. It is a "natural and original" property of the empassioned soul that it fixes on an idea of a particular kind. In the case of pride and humility, it is a natural and original property that the occurrence in the soul of either of these impressions of reflexion causes it to be actuated by the idea of the self. The connection between cause and passion is a natural but not original one. Pride is caused by the idea of the self possessing some laudable characteristic; humility, by the idea of the self as having some scurrilous feature. Love and hatred are structurally similar to pride and humility, the only difference being that the passion is brought about by the idea of the fine or odious qualities, respectively, of *another* thinking being. The passion causes the soul to focus on that other person. Accordingly, Hume designates the self as the object of pride and humility

---

[2] I believe it to be possible to give an adequate reconstruction of Hume's picture of the passions without demanding a reinterpretation of these notions as developed in Book I. I am aware that others have argued that Hume in Book II actually contravenes the tenets set out in Book I. For critical discussions of this point, see A. Baier, "Hume's Analysis of Pride"; D. Davidson, "Hume's Cognitive Theory of Pride"; and M. L. Wade, *Passion and Volition in Hume's 'Treatise'*. Most notable is the claim that Hume's picture of the passions presupposes the possibility of noncontingent empirical relations between distinct components. I do not agree with these critics, but to discuss the issue here would require too great a digression.

and the other individual as the object of love and hatred. Hume gives a less systematic and less thorough account of envy and malice, concluding that the object of these passions is the superior enjoyment of another individual.

In claiming that it is a natural property of the soul that certain emotions cause its views to focus on certain ideas, Hume asserts a lawlike connection between the passion and its object—they are constantly conjoined. His claim that the passion's conjuction with the object is original is the claim that, to use a more modern metaphor, the connection is "hard wired." Phrases like "primary constitution"[3] reinforce the idea of a parallel between Hume's notion of an original property of the mind and one that today is called an "innate" feature of the mind. I should stress that these are my own interpretations, not directly corroborated in Hume's text. In many places in the *Treatise*, Hume uses the term "natural" to designate a contrast with the "philosophical," suggesting that "natural" means no more than factual or empirical. I think there is more to it in the context of his discussion of the passions than this. Others have discussed the problematic nature of Hume's notions of "natural and original." I say no more about these here.[4]

It is a cornerstone of Hume's position that the cause and object of an emotion are distinct. As we have seen, the passions occur "betwixt that idea, which excites them, and that to which they direct their views when excited."[5] In pride, for example, the passion causes the soul to focus on the idea of self but it is not the idea of self that *causes* the soul to become thus ompassioned. It is the idea of one's possessing a laudable or pleasure-giving quality that excites the passion. Love and esteem are caused by ideas of another's virtues: "knowledge, wit, good sense" and good humor. The opposite passions of hatred and contempt are caused by these qualities' contraries.[6] The object of these emotions is the other person *simpliciter*. The cause of envy is the idea of the diminished worth of one's own goods seen in comparison with those of another.

Consider the following passage in which Hume describes his theory of pride and humility:

> We must, therefore, make a distinction betwixt the cause and the object of these passions, betwixt that idea which excites them, and

---

[3] Hume*op. cit.*, p. 281.

[4] See especially M. L. Wade, *op. cit.*

[5] Hume, *op. cit.* p.278.

[6] *ibid.* p.330.

that to which they direct their view, when excited... The first idea, that is presented to the mind, is that of the cause or productive principle. This excites the passion, connected with it; and that passion, when excited, turns our view to another idea... The first idea, therefore, represents the *cause*, the second the *object* of the passion.[7]

It is important to notice that even if one agrees with the claims of the above passage they are not sufficient alone to establish the fact that cause and object are distinct. We are only told that there are distinct *ideas* preceding and following the passions. The causes and objects of the passions are not the ideas that cause and are caused by the passions but those items in the world represented in these ideas—what the ideas are *of*. There is evidence for this interpretation in the passage above in "the first idea, therefore *represents* the cause, the second the *object* of the passion." Distinct ideas might be ideas *of* a common object. Hume rejects the possibility that the *ideas* converge; that is, represent the same thing. This convergence would amount to the identification of cause with object. Identifying the cause and object in the case of pride might lead one to claim that the idea of the self causes the soul's becoming actuated with pride, which in turn leads it to focus on the self.

Hume counters the possibility of identical causes and objects with a delightful argument. He makes use of this argument in discussing pride and humility, repeating it in his discussion of love and hatred. Here it is as it first appears:

But tho' that connected succession of perception, which we call the *self*, be always the object of these two passions, 'tis impossible it can be their CAUSE, or be sufficient alone to excite them. For as these passions are directly contrary, and have the same object in common; were their object also their cause, it cou'd never produce any degree of the one passion, but at the same time it must excite an equal degree of the other, which opposition and contrariety must destroy both.[8]

---

[7]   *ibid.* p.278.

[8]   *ibid.*,pp. 277-278.

The cause of each of the passions of pride and humility must be "something, which is peculiar to one of the passions, and produces not both in the very same degree."[9]

Reviewing Hume's argument, I find that it rests on the following suppositions: (i) that cause, or rather our conception of a cause, includes the condition that, ceterus paribus, a cause is "sufficient to excite" its effect; (ii) that pride and humility, being contrary passions, if occurring simultaneously in the same soul cancel each other; and (iii) that pride and humility have the same object as each other, the self. Hume then raises the question as to whether it could be the case that the self is both the object and cause of these emotions. His answer: No. Were the self the cause, it would be a sufficient condition for the arousal of both passions in the soul, by supposition (i). Given the supposition of the contrariety of pride and humility [i.e., (ii)], it would be impossible for either of these passions to be aroused. But we observe that these passions do, in fact, actuate the soul, which contradicts the conclusion that follows from the assumption that the self is the cause as well as the object. Therefore, the objects of pride and humility and their causes are distinct.

Setting aside the question of the merit of Hume's *argument,* it is worth noting the theoretical position it supports. It is not only a matter of fact that the cause and object are distinct but also a consequence of differences in their respective conceptions. That is, the cause and object are distinct because of distinct sets of conditions placed upon them by the notions of cause and object. Hume's argument against the identification of object with cause assumes the fact that, ceteris paribus, a cause is a sufficient condition for its effect. Were the object and cause identical, pride and humility could not occur independently of each other because they share the same object.[10]

It appears that Hume's argument suggests a weaker conclusion, too, that reflects on an object's explanatory power. Citing a sufficient condition, in particular, a cause, is generally considered a good form of explanation. Yet to require that any explanatory factor be sufficient is far too limiting

---

[9] *ibid.,* p.278.

[10] Complications are introduced when one begins to consider some of the ways philosophers have extended the notion of 'cause' to cover not only *the* cause, but also the entire range of causal factors or even enabling conditions. In doing so we lose the ceteris paribus sufficiency. My discussion is limited to consideration of factors that warrant the label "the cause."

on our notion of explanation. However, one would not judge something a legitimate explanatory factor if that factor served in the same way to explain a contrary event. Therefore, the basic framework of Hume's argument would lead to the conclusion that the object of an emotion is not an explanatory factor with respect to the emotion. This point distinguishes Hume's view from certain others on objects of emotion that insist on their explanatory worth.

It is surprising that Hume does not draw attention to the structural differences between the nature of causes and the nature of objects of emotions. The objects of pride, humility, love, and hatred are individual persons. The causes of these passions are more complex entities. Hume points out that there are two discernible components of the causes of passions. One is the "*quality* which operates" and the other is the "*subject*, on which it is placed."[11] Both elements must be present in the appropriate form in order that the passion be actuated in the soul. Beauty is an operative quality, but it will bring about pride only if it is the beauty of the self or of a possession of the self. Beauty considered alone does not arouse passion; the beauty of another may arouse love but does not arouse pride. The cause of a passion is a subject's *having* a particular quality or the *fact* that a certain subject has a certain quality. Because of their differing ontological categories, it would not make sense to suggest that the object of its emotion is its cause.

Hume's idea of the nature of object directedness covers only a fraction of the domain of the four conditions discussed in the first chapter. It incorporates the relationality condition because it posits that the object of an emotion stands in a particular relation to the individual's having an emotion. Having the emotion brings the idea of the emotion's object into the individual's consciousness. An instance of love, for example, is object directed if it involves another individual on whom one's view fixes when one is actuated with the passion. The condition requiring the object to have explanatory power with respect to the emotion is not incorporated into Hume's view. In fact, the contrary is strongly suggested, according to my interpretation. The same goes for the linguistic condition. Linguistic factors do not feature critically in Hume's account of the objects of emotions. The self being the object of pride is a metaphysical constraint that need not be reflected in the way one describes any instance of it. This is evidenced in one of Hume's examples in which "a man may be proud of his beauty, strength, good mein, address in dancing, riding, fencing and his

---

[11] Hume, *op. cit.*, p. 279.

dexterity in any manual business or manufacture."[12] The fact that the list of qualities follows the phrase "proud of" does not bear on the question of the object of the emotion.

A general remark about Hume's account of emotion's object directedness is that it involves an explicit empirical hypothesis. An object-directed emotion is one that consistently directs the view to an object in the world of a certain type. A priori considerations might suggest to us, for a given passion, whether it is object directed and, if so, what the object is, but the final test is empirical (despite what interpreters have said to challenge this). This feature of Hume's position makes a sharp contrast with the views on the object directedness of emotion put forward by a contemporary expositor, Anthony Kenny, whose work on emotion is among the most widely cited in the field.

2. Kenny

As is the case in Hume's views on the objects of emotion, it would be misleading, if not impossible, to present Kenny's views on emotion's object directedness independently of his views on the nature of emotion. In this section, I describe Kenny's account of emotion's object directedness, focusing on those of its features that distinguish it from other accounts and those most relevant to the way I have structured the domain. I include a critical appraisal of certain aspects of Kenny's position with further critical commentary in the following chapter.

In directing his readers to the phenomenon of emotion's object directedness, Kenny adopts the usual ploy of indicating the pervasiveness of directed emotions. In particular in using the directedness of emotion to distinguish emotions from sensations, Kenny writes, "Emotions, unlike pain, have objects: we are afraid *of* things, angry *with* people, ashamed *that* we have done such-and-such."[13] Though he draws initially on the intuitive underpinnings of object directedness, Kenny ends with an analyzed notion

---

[12] *Ibid.*, p. 279.

[13] A. Kenny, *Action, Emotion and Will*, p. 14.

that does not capture these early insights.[14] Moreover the analysis suffers serious internal flaws.

Kenny's position is frequently seen to include the following characteristic claims about object directedness. One is that emotions are universally object directed; another, that the question about the nature of an emotion's object is reducible to a question about the interpretation of certain linguistic expressions; a third, that the relation between emotion and object is noncontingent; and a fourth, an explicit commitment to debunking the possibility of a causal analysis of object directedness. I examine these claims critically, dwelling on a question that no other commentators have bothered with: whether Kenny's claims are consistent with one another.

Universality.   All emotions are object directed. One may legitimately expect an answer to the question, about every instance of emotion, "What is this emotion's object?" Since object directedness is seen to be a universal feature of emotions, it can be used in the definition of our conception of emotion. It does not serve as the basis for a sufficient condition because it does not distinguish emotions from other directed mental acts such as knowings and believings. It does, however, distinguish emotion from mere sensation, including pain, hunger, dizziness, and nausea. Kenny writes:

> The most important difference between a sensation and an emotion is that emotions, unlike sensations, are essentially directed to objects. It is possible to be hungry without being hungry for anything in particular, as it is not possible to be ashamed without being ashamed of anything in particular. [15]

---

[14] Throughout *Action, Emotion and Will* Kenny uses the phrases "object of emotion," "object directedness of emotion," "the relation or connection of emotion to object," and "the intensionality of emotion" interchangeably to pick out only one feature of emotion. Two of these locutions are anomalous. First, the suggestion of an emotion-object relation is inconsistent with his own nonrelational conception of emotion's object directedness. This seems a holdover from the intuitive conception. Second, "intensionality" as opposed to "intentionality" is inappropriate in light of more recent discussions of these terms. Intensionality is a notion that is seen to apply strictly to linguistic expressions; intentionality is its metaphysical counterpart. Kenny misses this distinction. Wilson, too, points out the confusion. I shall systematically use "t" to replace "s" where this is appropriate, except in direct quotation from Kenny.

[15] *Ibid.*, p. 60.

It is not important to my interests to evaluate Kenny's universality hypothesis except as it bears on the other aspects of his position on the nature of the objects of emotion. I return to this question below.

Objects and Grammar. As mentioned before, Kenny's initial introduction of the notion of the object directedness of emotion involves a demonstration of the usual sorts of convincing cases: loving and loathing *someone*, fearing *something*, and so forth. Later, however, he makes a bold effort to disassociate the notion of an object as used in this context with the idea of an object as a thing. The proper analysis of object directedness is not achieved by considering what type of 'thing' the object of an emotion is. The use of the term "object" that is critical to understanding the notion of "object of emotion" is found in the context of grammatical appraisals of sentences about emotions. In saying that emotions have objects, one indicates nothing more than the fact that emotion verbs are transitive or at least precede object expressions. The proper analysis of object directedness of emotion derives from an examination of the functioning of these object expressions in sentences containing emotion verbs. (From now on, for greater convenience in the discussion that follows, I use the term "emotion sentence" to cover the range of sentences that contain a transitive emotion verb and an object expression.) Kenny makes this point in the following passage:

> The sense of "object" which I have hitherto employed and wish now to discuss is one which derives from the grammatical notion of the *object* of the transitive verb. The object of fear is *what* is feared, the object of love is *what* is loved, the object of cutting is *what* is cut... In discussing the nature of objects we are simply discussing the logical role of the object-expression which completes the sense of the intensional and non-intensional verbs.[16]

This passage brings out several noteworthy points. Instead of asking directly the question "What are emotions' objects?" one asks about the functioning of certain expressions in emotion sentences. Kenny calls this a question about the "logical role" of the object expression. I interpret this as a concern with object expressions insofar as they affect the truth of the sentences in which they are embedded. In other words, Kenny reduces the question about the nature of the objects of emotion to a question about interpreting object expressions embedded in emotion sentences.

---

[16] *Ibid.*, pp. 187–188.

Kenny shares Brentano's view in claiming that the objects of emotions are not real items in the world.[17]   But his commitment to a linguistic condition and his explicit recognition of the structural similarities between sentences such as "He cut the cake" and "He hated the murderer," quite strongly suggest a relational interpretation of emotion sentences. Kenny must be able to reconcile these apparently conflicting factors. He employs the distinction between intensional and nonintensional verbs to drive a wedge between emotion sentences and other sentences involving transitive but nonintensional verbs.

Kenny devotes considerable attention to the distinction between intensional and nonintensional verbs, the aim being a distinction that will include all psychological verbs under the heading "intensional" and all others under the heading "nonintensional." One follows different rules when interpreting a sentence containing a transitive intensional verb from those one follows when interpreting a sentence containing a nonintensional verb. The need for distinct sets of rules is indicated in comparing sentences like "Last year her hair was red" and "He thought her hair was red." Kenny is convinced that if the criteria could be found that would successfully distinguish the category of the intensional from the category of the nonintensional, emotion verbs would fall in the former. In fact, Kenny's position rests on this assumption because he wants to avoid having to treat emotion verbs like action verbs and, likewise, their objects.

After evaluating several suggestions on how to draw the distinction, Kenny settles for three conditions offered by Chisholm. The conditions are, roughly: (i) Given an intensional sentence, neither it nor its contradiction implies the existence of referents for noun phrases occurring within the context of the intensional verb; (ii) one cannot substitute coreferential expressions in an intensional context *salva veritate*; and (iii) the truth value of an embedded sentence in an intensional context is independent of the truth value of the entire sentence.[18] This decision is disappointing because, as Kenny himself points out, Chisholm's conditions fail to classify as intensional the vital set of cases. The conditions successfully classify psychological verbs like "believes" and "desires" but fail to distinguish cases like "hates" from "cuts," which is clearly nonintensional. Realizing this failure, Kenny tries to prop up Chisholm's position with a condition he

---

[17] Perhaps this is a bit too simplistically taken, but it should serve the point I want to make quite fairly.

[18] See Kenny, *op. cit.* especially pp. 196–202 for a discussion of this issue.

attributes to the Medieval Schoolmen. The added condition is: An act is intentional if it brings about a change in its object; otherwise, it is not. The corresponding verb is intensional. But even this is unsuccessful, since there are clear cases of nonintentional acts like "climbing Mount Everest" in which the action brings about no change in its object. It somewhat undermines Kenny's enterprise that a distinction so crucial to his approach cannot be successfully supported.

I continue my discussion of Kenny's theory as if he had succeeded in justifying rules for the interpretation of emotion sentences that are distinct from those used in sentences containing other types of transitive verbs. It is not sufficient merely to establish a distinction between intensional and nonintensional verbs without showing precisely how this affects the interpretation of sentences containing emotion verbs and, further, how this bears on the question of emotion's objects. Kenny gives only a vague indication of how one is to interpret sentences containing emotion verbs and object expressions, despite the importance of this issue to his position. I attempt to round out Kenny's position by extending and adding details to his account in the most natural manner possible. Before doing so, I introduce stipulations on the use of several frequently employed expressions.

Kenny asserts that the notion of object directedness is derived from the linguistic character of so-called emotion sentences. I limit the application of this label to sentences of the following form: noun phrase / emotion verb phrase / object expression. The noun phrase designates the individual who is having the emotion. By "emotion verb phrase" I mean either a simple emotion verb like "loves," "hates," and "loathes" or a complex phrase comprised of a copula verb and a predicate adjective as illustrated in "is afraid" and "was distressed." Although the label is slightly misleading, I continue to use the term "emotion verb" to refer to both these cases. There is even greater variation in the possible form of the object expression. It covers proper names, definite and indefinite descriptions, prepositional phrases and clauses, *that*-clauses, and even *because*-clauses. Here are some examples of emotion sentences: "Bill loves Mary," "Joe despises his landlord," "Sam was fearful of being mugged in Central Park," "Tracy regretted that she hurt Molly's feelings," and "Ellen was delighted about her son's award." Also included are cases like "He was angry because I burst in without knocking" and "Tom was disgusted by conditions in the slum."

Kenny's reformulation of the question about the nature of emotion's directedness stated in the terms introduced above is this: The *real* problem of emotion's object directedness is to discover the semantic role of an object expression following an emotion verb. The test of Kenny's commitment to this reformulation of the problem is to see whether his theoretical position can be described in terms of linguistic functioning: whether all his claims about the objects of emotion are translatable into claims about the "logical" role of an object expression. I make this one of the criteria for assessing the internal adequacy of Kenny's theory.

I noted that it is crucial to Kenny's solution that emotion verbs be judged intensional, thereby placing object expressions in intensional contexts. This fact is relevant to the way one interprets these expressions. Kenny thus ties the question of the object directedness of emotion to questions Frege raised about indirect reference. Kenny selects Geach's proposed semantics of "judging" as a model for interpreting emotion sentences.[19] He briefly indicates how Geach's ideas may be extended to "volition" but makes mere passing reference to their possible application in the case of emotion verbs. I must therefore only speculate how Kenny might have followed the ideas through in this domain.

Emotion sentences containing emotion verbs and object expressions describe an individual's emotional state. The nature of the state is determined by the type of the emotion, given by the emotion verb, and something that Kenny calls the "exercise" or manipulation of concepts. The type of the emotion is determined on the basis of various bodily and mental symptoms, voluntary actions, and the context in which these occur. The object expression serves to further specify this state by describing conceptual manipulations that accompany the emotion state. Kenny describes this conceptual manipulation as "mental assertion," or "mental commanding." The object expression occurring after an emotion verb refers to the content of the conceptual manipulations. We are not further informed on this notion of "conceptual manipulation." Consider how this might work for "Ellen is delighted that her son won the award." This sentence describes Ellen's emotional state as delight, determined to be so on the basis of bodily and mental symptoms (that she is smiling, feels good, is energetic), that she acts in certain ways (tells everyone about it, is cheerful at work), and the context of these phenomena (the fact that her son won the award or that the response follows her hearing of the good news). The clause "that her son won the award" classifies Ellen's manipulation of concepts. The object directedness of her delight does *not* consist in a relation between

---

[19]   Kenny cites P. T. Geach, *Mental Acts*, London, 1957.

her delighted state and the event of her son's winning the award. In other words, the object expression is not taken to refer to the event of her son's winning the award.

Noncontingency.   This feature of Kenny's account, though perhaps its most distinguishing mark, is extremely puzzling. Kenny states, "The connection between emotions and their objects is not a contingent one."[20] It is not clear how one is to interpret this statement nor how to ascertain the phenomenon he wishes it to capture. Because of Kenny's stated aversion to a relational interpretation of emotion's object directedness, a further issue must be considered: whether it is possible to reduce his claims about the noncontingent connection between an emotion and its objects to a claim about the functioning of object expressions in emotion sentences.[21]

One way to interpret Kenny's claim that emotions are not contingently tied to their objects is as the claim that the concept of emotion precludes the possibility of an emotion with no object—a strong universality claim. The following passage, quoted earlier in full, indicates this interpretation:

> ...Emotions, unlike sensation, are essentially directed to objects.
> It is possible to be hungry without being hungry for anything in
> particular, as it is not possible to be ashamed without being ashamed
> of anything in particular.[22]

It supports the universality of object directedness because object directedness is tied into the concept of emotion. We cannot apply the concept of emotion to an experiential state unless it is a directed state. This enables one to conclude that all emotions have objects without having to gather empirical evidence in support of the claim. But there is no stronger suggestion about the tie between the nature of the object and the type of the emotion.

A different interpretation is suggested in another passage: "In fact each of the emotions is appropriate—logically and not just morally appropriate—

---

[20] *Ibid.*, p. 62.

[21] Kenny uses terms like "logical," "non-contingent," "conceptual," "essential," and "necessary," with no apparent appreciation of differences among them. I favor the term "conceptual" and shall on occasion use "noncontingent" or the phrase "not a mere matter of fact" but avoid more loaded terms like "logical" and "necessary." I rely on a certain nonrigorous understanding of the terms I employ.

[22] *Ibid.*, p. 60.

only to certain restricted objects."[23] To the position that all emotions are essentially object directed it adds that the connection between the *type* of an emotion and the *type* of an object is no mere matter of fact.

For Kenny's noncontingency hypothesis to make sense within the framework of his theory, one must consider how to translate it in terms of "logical functioning" of object expressions. This is difficult. To begin with, consider the weaker interpretation of noncontingency. The simplest translation, that every emotion verb must be followed by an object expression, is obviously infeasible. "Frank is angry" is a simple counterexample. A more promising possibility is to translate the hypothesis as the requirement that any occurrence of emotion *could* be described in terms of an emotion sentence that contains an object expression.

Thalberg, who also takes features of the way we *talk* about our emotions to be significant of their object directedness, reaches a conclusion that is at odds with this suggestion. On looking at the way we describe emotions, he concludes that not all emotions have objects. For example, hope and resentment are object directed, because "He hopes" and "He resents" *simpliciter* are impermissible and according to the dictates of grammar must be completed with object expressions. He concludes that emotions like hope and resentment must have objects. Emotions like embarrassment and delight *may* have objects because, though it is permissible according to the rules of grammar to say, "He is embarrassed" or "He is delighted," we expect there to be answers to questions like "What is he embarrassed about?" or "What is he delighted about?" In the case of depression or euphoria, however, we do not expect that there always be something that an individual is depressed or euphoric about. Therefore, Thalberg concludes that these emotions have no object.[24] This not only challenges the weak interpretation of the noncontingency claim but also the accuracy of the universality hypothesis.

The stronger noncontingency hypothesis is even more problematic when one considers what it might mean as a hypothesis about the "logical role" of object expressions in emotion sentences. First, consider Kenny's motivation for positing a noncontingent connection between certain types of emotions and certain types of objects. Kenny notices that certain object expressions are especially fitting to certain types of emotions. "Fearing

---

[23]   *Ibid.*, p. 192.

[24]   See I. Thalberg, "Emotion and Thought," in *Philosophy of Mind*, S. Hampshire (Ed.).

future evils" and "envying *the possessions of another*" are examples of this. Conversely, certain object expressions are particularly unfitting, as, for example, being grateful *for harm done to one* or angered *by benefit accrued.*[25] This launches Kenny into a discussion of the "formal objects" of emotion in which he claims that the formal object of fear, for example, is a future evil. I avoid the use of "formal object" since it diverts attention to the question of the ontological nature of these mysterious objects. I think I am being fair to Kenny's position in replacing talk about formal objects with talk of conceptual ties. Kenny goes further than noting a "good fit" between certain types of emotions and certain types of objects. The connection is conceptual. It is a conceptual consequence of someone's fearing that the person fears a future evil. The concept of anger precludes a situation in which a person is angry over benefit accrued. In general, a conceptual consequence of an emotion's being of a certain type is that its object is of a certain type.

I do not intend to evaluate, in its own right, the position according to which the type of the emotion is conceptually tied to the type of its objects. I examine here the viability of the position within the framework of Kenny's theory. The problem is to try to interpret the noncontingency claim as a claim about emotion verbs and object expressions. I argue that unless one takes considerable liberty interpreting Kenny's noncontingency claim, his position is untenable.

Take the case of an individual, Sam, who fears something. Kenny insists that it is a conceptual consequence of Sam's fearing that he fears a future evil. Interpreting this as an assertion about the functioning of linguistic expressions, one might say that the *sentence* "Sam fears a future evil" is a conceptual consequence of "Sam fears" or that "If Sam fears then he fears, a future evil" is conceptually true. The sentence describes Sam's emotional state, which involves his manipulating the concepts in "future evil." The label "fear" applies to Sam's state only if the state is of the right type and Sam is engaged in the appropriate concept manipulation. Consider the

---

[25] Kenny stipulates that, strictly speaking, these should be fearing what the subject believes to be a future evil, being angry over what the subject believes to be a benefit accrued, etc. For simplicity, these qualifiers are omitted. Actually, I think Kenny belies a confusion by inserting this stipulation, since emotion verbs' being intensional ensures the appropriate "mental assertion." This kind of switching back and forth between relational and nonrelational paradigms is evidenced throughout his book.

assertion "Jim fears being mugged in Central Park," a plausible example of an emotion sentence. This straightforward example appears to constitute a refutation to Kenny's claim. Kenny asserts that *all* objects are conceptually connected to the emotions that are directed to them, but "being mugged in Central Park" is surely not part of the concept of fear. This is therefore an instance of an emotion that is only contingently tied to its object.

Not so, one might say. According to Kenny's psychology, Jim's fear state involves Jim in the manipulation of the conceptual content of "being mugged in Central Park." But since Jim's experience is a case of fear, it is conceptually required that it be a case of fearing a future evil. Being mugged in Central Park is perceived by Jim to be a future evil (see previous footnote); therefore, it is conceptually true that Jim fears being mugged in Central Park. In other words, one may describe Jim's state by either "Jim fears a future evil" or "Jim fears being mugged in Central Park." And because the former is conceptually true, so is the latter—thus supporting Kenny's claim that the connection between an emotion and its object is not contingent.

The conclusion, that it is a consequence of our concept of fear that Sam fears being mugged in Central Park, is unacceptable, and the argument is invalid. The fact that the two sentences describe a common state of the world does not permit their identification along all dimensions. In particular, we may not, on the basis of their referential functions, draw conclusions about their conceptual features. Frege drew attention to this fact in his puzzle about identity statements. "Jim fears a future evil" being true by virtue of the concepts involved is a fact about the *meanings* of the terms used in that sentence. This gives us no reason to conclude that the coreferential "Jim fears being mugged in Central Park" has a similar conceptual feature.

It might follow from the concept of fear that one fears only future evils or from the concept of anger that one does not become angry over being benefited. The problem is that there seems to be no way to support this claim in terms of Kenny's reduction of the emotion-object relation in terms of emotion verbs and any object expressions. Even if it is "mere matter of fact" that people are not angered by being benefited nor fear the glorious past, fearing being mugged in Central Park and not becoming angry over an exceptional job promotion are no more consequences of our concepts than "the fact that most people are nauseated by slugs crawling from beneath an upturned stone and sneeze on getting pepper in their noses" is.[26] Kenny cites the last two cases to contrast contingent, though regularly connected, stimulus-response patterns from ones that reflect conceptual underpinnings. But the mugging and job promotion cases seem, on Kenny's view, to have equal status to the first two examples.

The claim that the emotions are "essentially directed" to their objects—that the connection between emotion and object is not contingent—features prominently throughout Kenny's account of emotion's object directedness. While others have either conceded this point or argued against it, saying that it does not make sense to claim noncontingent relations between things in the world,[27] I have been concerned to interpret Kenny's claim in terms of his stated reduction of the issue of object directedness of emotion to an issue about the role of certain expressions in emotion sentences. I have argued that, given Kenny's commitment to seeing the notion of an object of emotion in this way, the non contingency hypothesis is insupportable. The insight Kenny demonstrates in bringing to bear the idea of a formal object on the object directedness of emotions draws our attention to certain—perhaps valid—conceptual ties between emotion terms and other expressions, between the type of the emotion and the type of the object. I have argued that Kenny's sweeping noncontingency claim finds no straightforward counterpart that satisfies the linguistic condition he adopts.

One might try to defend Kenny's noncontingency claim by employing more imaginative ways of interpreting it as a claim about emotion sentences.[28] Further, reinterpreting the noncontingency claim within a completely different metaphysical framework might give it greater plausibility. In fact, in the view I eventually adopt there is an implicit conceptual link between the type of the emotion and the nature of the object. My argument has been explicitly directed against the noncontingency claim considered in the light of Kenny's other theses.

---

[26] *Ibid.*, p. 192.

[27] See J. R. S. Wilson, *Emotion and Object.*

[28] Michael Bratman suggested that one might try bringing in the conceptual tie between an emotion and its object by asserting that "Jim fears being mugged in Central Park" conceptually implies "Jim believes that being mugged in Central Park is a future evil." Whatever Jim fears, it is conceptually implied that he believes it to be a future evil.

Against a Causal Analysis.   I discuss two of Kenny's arguments against the possibility of a successful causal analysis of object directedness. One of these shows no more than that a causal analysis conflicts with Kenny's own doctrine. According to Humean doctrine, a causal relation is contingent while the emotion object relation is not. Second, if one follows Kenny's approach to the question through language and takes emotion verbs to be intensional, the emotion object relation is not a relation at all. That is, since emotion sentences do not describe real relations, they could hardly be given as descriptions of causal relations. These arguments carry weight *only if* one accepts Kenny's noncontingency thesis and his way of interpreting object expressions following emotion verbs, which precludes a relational analysis of object directedness.

The second argument against the possibility of a causal analysis is independent of Kenny's own position on object directedness. A typical causal analysis takes a case like "Hannah was angry that she had not been invited to the party" and suggests that Hannah's not being invited to the party, an event, is the object of her anger in that it plays a causal role in her being angry. Kenny argues that, since many object expressions in emotion sentences refer to future or possible occurrences, it makes no sense to suppose that object expressions designate causes of the emotions designated by the emotion terms. This fact is evidenced by such cases as fear, dread, and worry. Future-looking object expressions, as one finds in these cases, cannot *now* be taken to designate causal factors. Consider in this light the earlier example in which Jim fears being mugged in Central Park.

Proponents of a causal theory have suggested that the causal antecedent in question is not the actual event designated by the object expression but a mental image or, to use a more up-to-date metaphor, a mental representation of the present, future, or possible event.[29] Kenny rejects this move, saying that taking the image or mental representation to be the emotion's object does not square with the intuitive ideas grounding the notion of objects of emotion. After all, no one dreads or fears or is apprehensive of an

---

[29]   This sort of move is often suggested by psychologists (George Mandler and Phoebe Ellsworth, in conversation) wishing to fit object directedness into a stimulus-response model. Descartes, though not explicitly acknowledging emotion's object directedness, could be seen as suggesting a variant of this view when he describes the way an image of a loved one serves to sustain the passion of love; See *The Passions of the Soul*, Book II, Article 120, transl. Stephen Voss, Unpublished manuscript.

image. Kenny presents us with a dilemma. We can either save the causal analysis by positing images as causes and objects and abandon the idea of an object of an emotion as *what* one fears, dreads, and so forth, or save the intuition and forgo the causal analysis. Kenny clearly favors the second alternative, which I describe further in the next section. I show later that Wilson offers a third alternative.[30]

Summary.   Kenny's notion of object directedness covers a wide base. All emotions have objects; in fact, this feature distinguishes emotion from other sensations. Kenny takes the notion of an object of emotion to be derivative of the grammatical category of objects of transitive verbs and not of the idea of an object as a thing in the world. The proper analysis of object directedness begins with a question about the referential properties of object expressions following emotion verbs, which according to Kenny are intensional verbs. The object expression in an emotion sentence serves to further specify the emotional state indicated by the emotion verb. The emotional state occurs in combination with mental manipulation of concepts designated by the object expression. The entire state is the object-directed emotion. There is no independently existing item in the world that is the emotion's object. The connection between an emotion and its object is not a contingent one.

Kenny's position incorporates two of the conditions I discuss in the first chapter: the linguistic condition and the intentional-state condition. Unfortunately, Kenny says very little on the interpretation he gives to "intentionality" aside from the the passage quoted from Brentano. Kenny explicitly denies the validity of the relational condition. The condition demanding the explanatory effectiveness of emotions' objects is neither directly supported nor dismissed by Kenny's theory.

Critical Remarks.   The remaining discussion is devoted to an evaluation of Kenny's position with a view to a more global appraisal of the notion of emotion's object directedness that he attempts to project. I focus on how it fares as a representative of a theoretical position that takes seriously the linguistic condition that is, a position that accepts the condition requiring an object-directed emotion to be the designatum of a certain type of linguistic expression. The gist of my appraisal is this: Kenny fails to realize the potential of the linguistic condition as a starting point in the investigation of object directedness. He makes two types of errors: one in

---

[30] J. R. S. Wilson, *op. cit.*

taking irrelevant linguistic features too seriously, the other in failing to give sufficient regard to potentially important structural features.

Kenny projects an overly simplistic picture of the linguistic structure of the expressions we use to describe and refer to our emotions. He deals with a limited set of categories: subject phrases, emotion verbs, and object expressions. The feature of emotion verbs that bears most significantly on his theory is their being intensional. This is partially responsible for both failings that I noted. For one thing, the variations in types of emotion expressions is far too great to allow so crude a classification. I return to this point later.

Kenny's choice leads him to commit an error of the first type as well, by stifling the effects of the object expression on total sentence meaning. One consequence is a calling into question of possible criteria for the individuation of emotions' objects. Take a case in which the subject, named Ella, is fearful of her neighbor's bullmastiff. It is also true that Ella is fearful of her neighbor's dog and her neighbor's pet. The question: how many objects of Ella's fear are there? If the neighbor's pet is a dog of the bullmastiff breed, a relational account might have no problem in providing the answer, "One." Perhaps this is not a fair question to put to a defender of Kenny's position. Possibly a better one is: "Do we have here three object-directed fear states or only one?" Kenny gives no basis for making the identification since it is reasonable to assume that each of the object expressions marks a unique manipulation of concepts. One is prevented from bringing to bear important matters of fact in determining the nature of Ella's fear and letting irrelevant linguistic factors determine one's judgments about its object.

A far greater problem is Kenny's neglect of variation among linguistic expressions that is significant to object directedness; that is, he fails to recognize differences that *do* make a difference. Kenny submerges under the label "object expression" a heterogeneous set of linguistic categories, including noun phrases—names, pronouns, event nominalizations, definite and indefinite descriptions; prepositional phrases and clauses; *that*-clauses; *because*-clauses; and many more.[31] Kenny explicitly disavows the relevance

---

[31] I have compiled a list of cases of emotion sentences with the emotion term occurring as a component of the verb phrase in order to get an idea of the diversity of our ways of talking about emotions. The list is very long and varied. See the Appendix for types of constructions not mentioned in this paragraph.

of variation in syntactic construction in object expressions. He denies that there are serious "logical" differences underlying the large number of variations in the way one may report on an affective attitude. He writes:

> The proliferation of different constructions after affective verbs in English can hardly be of logical importance, since no two languages seem to agree on the analogies which they draw between reports of different kinds.[32]

To support this sweeping disclaimer, Kenny offers only one example of the disanalogy between English and Latin in the constructions associated with the verbs "want" and "volo," respectively. Kenny makes a similar point in the passage below in which he argues that differences in the way we describe an emotion's object directedness do not signal semantic or, to use his term, "logical" differences but merely exemplify the diversity of the idiom:

> Thus, we may say "I was angry with him, not because of what he said, but because of the way he spoke" or "I was angry at his way of speaking, not at what he said" or "It was the way he spoke, not what he said, that made me angry".[33]

I argue contrary to Kenny that one cannot pass off these differences as differences in mere idiom with no semantic significance and therefore with no significance for object directedness. Consider the two assertions: (i) Bill was angry at Mary because she went to the movie with Steve and (ii) Bill was angry because Mary went to the movie with Steve. Whether one follows Kenny in seeing emotion's object directedness as a complex feature of the person experiencing the emotion *or* gives a relational analysis of directedness, the difference between (i) and (ii) is of significance, because they express distinct facts about Bill's directed anger. Mary is the object of Bill's anger in (i), given a relational interpretation. In (ii) it is quite conceivable that Bill is *not* angry at Mary at all.

Here is another example requiring a finer attention to language than Kenny is prepared to allow. Consider: (i) Erica is afraid of being beaten and robbed and (ii) Terry is afraid that he will be beaten and robbed.[34] These assertions are significantly different from each other. Erica and Terry

---

[32] Kenny. *op.cit.*, p. 214.

[33] *Ibid.*, p. 74.

[34] Jon Barwise drew my attention to these types of cases.

are walking across the Quad at eleven o'clock on a Monday morning, (i) and (ii) being true at that location. Erica's emotional attitude is perfectly acceptable. It is "normal" to fear being robbed and beaten. Yet one might be inclined to suggest to Terry that he speak to someone about his tendency to paranoia. The subjects' fears do not have a common object. Language affords us the capability of drawing these subtle distinctions, which should not be passed off as mere idiom.

Let us return to one of Kenny's arguments against the possibility of a causal analysis of the notion of an object of emotion. In this instance, too, I accuse Kenny of not taking language seriously enough. The observation behind the argument is that if the object expression following certain emotion verbs is future looking, or refers to a possible event only, it can hardly be said to designate a component of the emotion's cause. We can turn this argument on its head, for it rests on the assumption Kenny makes—and which I am now challenging—that there is a single right way to interpret the role of object expressions in emotion sentences. A causal analysis is a priori in jeopardy only if one expects a universal rule for interpreting object expressions, irrespective of structural differences among them. A proponent of a causal analysis, noting precisely the features Kenny notes (future and possible cases), draws a quite different conclusion: Objects are causal factors, which only goes to show that the 'difficult' statements do not express an emotion object relation. He uses linguistic markers such as tense and modals to delineate positive cases, concluding on these grounds that the emotions described in statements like "Terry fears that he will be robbed and mugged" and "David is dreading seeing his ex-wife" are not object directed.

In the cases I discuss I try to draw attention to the fact that, if one is committed to an approach to object directedness through language, one cannot ignore variation in the object expression that makes a difference to the identification of an emotion's object. I conclude with a remark about the emotion verbs themselves. Kenny tries hard to lump together all emotion verbs under the classification "intensional verbs," using this as a license to relieve the object expressions of their usual referential function. Kenny has the insight to identify certain of the cases that prove troublesome for this classification. First, transitive emotion verbs taking direct objects, like loves, loathes, and despises, are not distinguishable on his conditions as intensional verbs. Second, there are cases of intensional verbs for which Kenny's non relational interpretation is inappropriate. Take, for example, the verb "knows" as it is used in "Bill knows Mary." Unlike many other verbs designating mental attitudes, this one does have existential implications. For Bill to know Mary, Mary must exist and must stand in a certain relation to Bill. Cases like these have made the definition of mental predicates extremely difficult. Likewise, emotions should not be treated as a homogeneous class. It may be true that a report of fearing a future evil has no current existential implications, yet this is not true of all emotion reports. If I report that Bill loves Mary, despises Joan, and loathes Betty, the information contained in these reports is not limited in content to Bill's emotional and cognitive states, because if Mary, Joan, and Betty were mere figments of Bill's imagination the reports would be false.

Conclusion.   Kenny's position on emotion's object directedness is known for several of its distinctive theses. The thesis that emotions are not contingently connected to their objects, given the other postulates of Kenny's position, is incoherent and well worth forgetting. I prefer not to take sides on the universality debate since it rests on agreement over what object directedness is, which is precisely the point being contended. In any case, the universality thesis is well challenged by depression, which is offered as an emotion that is not object directed. My main concern is the way Kenny incorporates the linguistic condition into his view. I criticize Kenny for interpreting this condition too simplistically, so that it fails to to be informative with respect to the notion of object directedness. A linguistic condition, in order to be enlightening, must be sensitive to linguistic variation. Kenny's is not. Whether or not the distinctions drawn in English are paralleled in other languages does not bear on the fact that they are relevant to the analysis of English sentences.

Perhaps an analogy will help underscore what I consider to be a major failing in Kenny's enterprise. An important factor in gaining deeper knowledge is the way the domain of an inquiry is defined. I doubt anyone would get very far in the study of things that were plants, red cubic objects, or insects that travel faster than fifteen miles per hour. It is unlikely they would discover interesting further conditions or laws that all members of the domain satisfy—besides the specification that defined the domain in the first place.

Kenny identifies the question of object directedness as a question about linguistic functioning. The only criterion for including cases in his domain of interest is that they be sentences containing emotion verbs and object expressions. I show that this criterion is not a sufficient one for the purpose of furthering our understanding of object directedness. The class of cases it defines is so diverse as to preclude the discovery of any further common features beyond their satisfaction of Kenny's original stipulation. And if, indeed, all that the sentences have in common is their inclusion of an emotion verb followed by an object expression, it is hard to see the source of our interest in the issue of emotion's object directedness.

3. Rorty and Solomon

One finds in the views expressed by Rorty and Solomon a common way of framing questions about emotion's object directedness, one that they share with Kenny. This framework is partially determined by an adherence to the intentional state condition. Each of the three authors approaches the issue of emotion's object directedness by considering the features of an emotional state (or experience) that are responsible for its being an intentional state. Like Kenny, Rorty and Solomon reject the idea that the object directedness of emotion consists in a certain type of relation between the emotion, or the individual's having the emotion, and an item in the world whose existence does not depend on the subject's mental state. Solomon and Rorty share the view that emotion's object directedness has something to do with the way we perceive the world. Finally, their views diverge sharply from Kenny's in not explicitly recognizing language as a primary factor in determining the nature of object directedness. Both Rorty and Solomon ignore the issue of the way language might contribute to the notion of object directedness and do not acknowledge the influence of linguistic phenomena in determining the nature of the notion. This complete neglect shows up in their views in their treatment of what are really facts about language as if they were facts of metaphysics. Before I begin with Rorty's view, I note that the source for this outline is a paper[35] that is not primarily directed to the issue of emotion's objects and in which only a relatively small part is devoted to the question.

Rorty.   Rorty characterizes her position on object directedness of emotion as a descendant of Hume's, whose view she considers to be the first in which the distinction between the object of an emotion and its cause is explicitly drawn. Her view is a refinement of the one Hume presents. One faces a problem in attempting an outline of Rorty's view. If one pays close attention to the details of her presentation of it, one finds instances of

---

[35] A. Rorty, "Explaining Emotions," in *Explaining Emotions*, A. Rorty (ed.).

internal inconsistencies, with some parts that make no sense at all. On the other hand, if one takes liberty in interpreting some of the notions and ignores the errors, it is possible to use her revised view to illustrate a particular way of looking at emotion's object directedness. I have chosen the second alternative, attempting a reconstruction of her view. I point to some of the problems with Rorty's text and offer these as reasons for the changes I suggest. I conclude with a critical commentary.

According to Rorty, the object of an emotion is an abstract object: an intentional object. In Chapter 1 I established the two possible uses of the term "intentional object." One is theoretically neutral, picking out that to which a mental attitude is directed. The question "What is the intentional object of emotion?" is open-ended, implying no presuppositions of the object's metaphysical status. It could be a concrete particular, an idea, a linguistic entity, and so forth. The second use is metaphysically loaded and refers to a type of abstract object toward which emotions and other mental attitudes are directed. In the passage of Brentano's quoted in Chapter 1, this use is described. An intentional object is not a concrete particular nor is it, usually, a mental entity. I take Rorty to be using "intentional object" in the second sense. She writes:

> The immediate object of an emotion is characteristically intentional, directed and referring to objects under descriptions that cannot be substituted *salva affectione*. Standardly, the immediate object not only is the focus of the emotion but is also taken by the person as providing its ground or rationale.[36]

In some cases there is a concrete correlate of the object out in the world: its immediate target, "the object extensionally described and identified."[37] If one keeps in mind the noted parallels between the objects of emotion and of perception and the possibility in both of illusion, hallucination, and mistaken identity, one will readily agree that not all instances of object-directed emotion have targets and that it is a mistake to believe that the objects are concrete particulars.

---

[36] *Ibid.*, p. 107.

[37] Rorty, *op. cit.* From here on, I drop Rorty's qualifier "immediate." It is used effectively to distinguish two types of causes of emotions: immediate causes and significant causes. Since Rorty offers us no parallel notions of significant objects and targets, nothing is likely to be lost in simply dropping the qualifier in the case of these two items.

The first sentence in the passage quoted above is confusing in that it is unclear whether it states a fact about language or about the ontological character of intentional objects. Rorty says that an intentional object of emotion *refers* to some other object with descriptions that may not be substituted without effecting a change in the nature of the emotion. If an intentional object is not a linguistic expression of some kind, what sense is there to be made of its referring to an object? (Notice that she does not claim that it refers to the target, though this might make more sense.) Rorty gives no indication of the way descriptions—linguistic expressions—enter the picture. The descriptions may not be substituted without affecting the nature of the emotion, she claims. Substituted in *what*, with what? Denying the propriety of substitution presupposes a context of substitution. If one is substituting descriptions, this suggests a linguistic context. Rorty offers no insight into the relation of intentional objects to language. One may suppose that Rorty's idea of no substitution *salva affectione* draws on, and is intended as, an extension of the stipulation made for other cognitive attitudes: no substitutivity in intensional contexts *salva veritate*. Yet, in its widely accepted form, this claim is one about the properties of *linguistic* contexts.

I offer the following suggestion of a view Rorty might have intended with that garbled sentence: An intentional object is a complex abstract entity whose components are properties. In a given instance of an object-directed emotion, the intentional object is comprised of those properties that the subject of the emotion attributes to a concrete particular: individual, event, or state of affairs. Consider the example of Lynne, driving for the first time in Manhattan. She is about to back into a parking space when someone roars up from behind and steals it from her. The object of Lynne's anger consists of a complex of the following properties: male, brown hair, balding, unattractive, drives a red Porsche, stole the parking space on Bleecker Street that had taken an hour to find, uncouth, rude, unscrupulous. In fact, the individual was driving a Datsun ZX, was wearing plaid polyester pants, is the most respected classicist in New York City, and is an outspoken proponent of civil rights.

The interrelation between intentional object and target (an extended object) is complex. According to Rorty, the intentional object of emotion refers to an extended object. The intentional object of Lynne's anger refers to the individual, the classicist. It is reasonable to wonder how one would define this relation—perhaps on the basis of matching properties, subject's dispositions, and so forth. But the second part of Rorty's sentence is as mysterious as the first. We might be able to shed light on it by considering once more these intentional complexes of properties. Since the intentional object of Lynne's anger is comprised of only those properties that she attributes to it, this restricts the descriptions that apply to it—namely those only that designate a property in the intentional object. One cannot substitute for one of these descriptions a description that applies only to the target. In identifying the individual who stole the parking space one may use "the most respected classicist in New York City" or "the man wearing plaid polyester pants." Neither of these would designate the intentional object of Lynne's anger.

This does not quite explain Rorty's claim preventing substitutivity *salva affectione*. Object directedness of emotion is analyzed as a relation between an individual, or an individual's emotional state, and an intentional object. Consider:

1. Lynne is angry at the man who stole her parking space.

This statement describes an instance of object-directed anger. The object according to Rorty is intentional and is supposedly designated by "the man who stole her parking space." Rorty's view should sanction as truth-preserving the substitution of any other description that refers to the intentional object of Lynne's anger. Thus,

2. Lynne is angry at the brown-haired man.

is a valid outcome of the substitution.

"Intentional object" comes out in this interpretation as an analogue of Frege's "sense," supporting the usual constraints on substitutability in intensional contexts. But why not be satisfied with truth-preserving substitutability? Why does Rorty want the substitution to be affect-preserving, and what could she mean by this? I suspect Rorty would not agree that statement 2 is affect-preserving.

I suggested that the intentional object of an emotion is comprised of *all* the features attributed to it by the emoting subject. Perhaps this is not so. Perhaps the intentional object includes only those properties that are *relevant* to the emotion. One maintains the principle of substitutability but alters the emotion's object. This way statement 2 is not offered as a substitution instance of 1. The next question should be obvious: What features are emotionally relevant features? That is, how may we know what the intentional object consists of? The intentional object of Lynne's anger might include only the property designated by "the individual who stole the much sought after parking space." That is, whether or not Lynne knows that the individual is the most respected classicist in New York City or an outspoken proponent of civil rights—a cause she happens to support—the intentional object of anger includes none of these properties. The question is whether there is some principled way of determining the intentional object of an emotion. After all, this is precisely what one might expect a successful analysis to provide. Although obscure, the second sentence of the quoted passage gives a clue to a possible answer.

Rorty asserts that the object both is the focus of and is taken by the person to provide the grounds or rationale for the emotion. (I use the term "reasons" in place of "grounds" or "rationale" for greater convenience. I do not believe this alters the point significantly.) This reason-giving capacity of the object provides an answer to the question raised above about emotionally relevant features. In citing the reason for something, an action, an attitude, an emotion,[38] one is giving an explanation of the phenomenon, albeit an explanation of a special type. If, in citing the object, the person cites her reason for the emotion, then the object has explanatory power with respect to the emotion. The implications of this conclusion are twofold. First, on the assumption that there is considerable uniformity across individuals in their reasons for emotions, it holds the key to a possible principle for determining the constituents of an intentional object. One easily imagines Lynne offering as a reason for her anger the fact that the man stole her parking space. The man's being an outspoken proponent of civil rights does not have the same reason-giving force. This assures the former a position as a constituent of Lynne's anger and not the latter. In general, only the emotionally relevant properties are included as components of the emotion's intentional object. The emotionally relevant properties of an item are those that have reason-giving force with respect to the emotion. I leave the matter here, hoping to have shed light on one part of Rorty's position. To follow the discussion further would require a deeper examination of the issue of explanation of emotion—which luckily, is outside the scope of my dissertation.

Second, having an emotion's object provide a rationale for the emotion constitutes a major divergence from Hume's picture of emotion's objects, rendering inaccurate the conception of Rorty's view as simply a refinement of Hume's. It is a fundamental tenet of Hume's analysis that there can be no systematic link between the object of an emotion and its explanation. If someone were to cite a phenomenon a in an explanation of an event

---

[38] I assume that it makes sense to talk of "reasons" for emotions, although I am aware that there is much controversy surrounding this issue.

e, and also cite *a* in an explanation of not-*e*, one would probably judge that the person had not understood the notion of an explanation. This is precisely the form of Hume's argument to show that the objects and causes of pride and humility are distinct. A Humean would argue along similar lines against Rorty's demand that an emotion is explained by its object. In suggesting that the object has reason-giving force, she contradicts one of Hume's most fundamental claims.

Rorty blurs the picture by requiring the object to be both ground-giving and the focus of the emotion, precisely the point Hume avoids in keeping the categories of "object" and "cause" distinct. In this I am in agreement with Hume. This point will be discussed at greater length in the following chapter, but I briefly express it here. Given the statement "Frank loves Susan" with no further information, it seems reasonable to claim that one knows the object (qua focus) of Frank's loving having no thoughts on Frank's reasons for his emotion. It is likely that Frank loves Susan in virtue of features he perceives her to have. Yet it seems sufficient to identify the individual, Susan, as the focus of love. Conversely, you might know the rationale for a person's emotion but not know what its focus is. Take the following statement: "I am angry because my effort and hard work were not rewarded." These cases are intended to show that our notions of an emotion's focus and the emotion's rationale do not converge.

Solomon.   One detects a shift over time in Solomon's views on the intentionality of emotion. One version of his account is similar to Rorty's in that it posits the existence of intentional objects with emotions directed towards these objects.[39] He offers little guidance on the supposed nature of these intentional objects except that they are "opaque." As with Rorty's picture, this indicates confusion of a linguistic feature with a metaphysical one. Perhaps Solomon means to say that an emotion verb, "is angry," for example, creates an opaque context. It is actually another version of Solomon's account that interests me more; therefore, I spend no more time considering this one.[40]

---

[39] For this version, see the main body of Solomon's paper "Emotion and Choice," in *Explaining Emotions*, A Rorty (ed.)

[40] The second version is found in the Appendix to Solomon, "Emotion and Choice," and in another paper, "Nothing to Be Proud of," in *Understanding Human Emotions*, Bowling Green Studies in Applied Philosophy, vol. I.

In the second version of Solomon's account, he argues that we will never understand emotion's intentionality if we begin the analysis by assuming that the emotion component is separable from the component we identify as the emotion's object. Hume's analysis is an example of this ill-fated approach. If one takes intentionality of emotion to cover a relation between an emotion and a concrete particular, cases of future-directed and nonveridical emotion challenge that position. This leads to views like Rorty's, which posit abstract objects of emotion. Solomon denies the relational nature of intentionality altogether. It gives no further insight to the problem to posit a range of mysterious existents to be one's objects of emotion. Emotion's intentionality is something to be found in the experience of the emotion alone. When one makes reference to an emotion's object, one is not referring to something that is separable from the emotion itself—as Hume's atomism would suggest—but one is simply giving a further description of the emotion. This claim echoes Kenny's position.[41]

I identify two components in Solomon's view on the intentionality of emotion that are especially characteristic of it. First, he is committed to the nonseparability of an emotion from its object. This distinguishes his view from any view that interprets intentionality in terms of an emotion-object *relation* irrespective of the ontological character of the object. Second, in a move that is unique to Solomon, he holds that an instance of an object-directed emotion is an "irreducible complex." Kenny, who also eschews a relational interpretation of object directedness, diverges from Solomon in allowing the components of the object expression to indicate a corresponding structure of conceptual components being manipulated in the mind.

Solomon advocates a complex experience as the unit of analysis of emotions. In place of the Humean model, Solomon wants

> to substitute an organic molecule, in our case of pride, the irreducible complex, *being-proud-of-my-house* ... *Being-proud-of-my-house* is, in Heidegger's terminology, a "unitary phenomenon." The so-called "object" is not simply *the house* but is defined by the emotion of which it is a part. Neither is being proud a distinctive psychological entity, "directed towards" or possibly even looking for an object.

---

[41] It is worth looking more closely at what the difference amounts to between a view that is formally relational, in which the object is an abstract construction, and a view that is touted as nonrelational but imposes the structure of directedness onto the intentional state.

Being-proud-of-my-house is a complex and irreducible experience,
not divisible into components or individual atoms.[42]

Solomon makes an unfortunate choice of metaphor in comparing an emotion
to an organic molecule and shortly afterward denying that it is divisible
into "individual atoms." Which are we supposed to believe? In any case,
Solomon's picture of emotion as a "system of judgments" is supposed to
provide the setting against which we grasp the nature of their intentionality
as an integral and unanalyzable part of an emotional experience. Emotions
are active ways of "structuring our experience."

I want to sidestep the issue of Solomon's theory of emotion and focus on
his proposal regarding emotion's intentionality. He urges that we abandon
a relational interpretation of a statement like "He is proud of his beautiful
house." If one allows the object expressions their usual referential function,
one fails to take into account the fact that the objects of emotion are objects
as perceived by individuals. The properties the individual ascribes to the
object need not be actual properties of the object. Moreover, the object
of emotion need not actually exist. On the other hand, Solomon sees no
benefit in creating a new realm of existents for the object expression to
refer to—intentional objects. The alternative he proposes is to take "proud
of his new house" to be a one-place predicate, so that the question of the
nature of a separate existent referred to by the expression "his beautiful
new house" simply does not arise.

This parallels the solution Quine proposes to the problem of the objects of belief and how one interprets expressions following "believes" and
other propositional attitude verbs. He writes, "Hence a final alternative
that I find as appealing as any is simply to dispense with the objects of
the propositional attitudes."[43] The form of the sentence "Tom believes
Cicero denounced Cataline" is not 'Fab', but 'Fa' with 'F' the complex
predicate 'believes-Cicero-denounced-Cataline'. This dispenses with objects of propositional attitudes because one no longer interprets "believes"
relationally.

My reasons for finding Solomon's move objectionable are similar to ones
Davidson offers in objection to Quine's proposal.[44] The structural features
of the complex predicate should not be ignored, since frequently they reflect

---

[42] R. C. Solomon, "Nothing to Be Proud of," p. 31.

[43] W. V. O. Quine, *Word and Object*, p. 216.

[44] In D. Davidson, "On Saying That," in *Synthese*, 1968-69.

significant semantic features. The cost of Solomon's move is that it blocks
the obvious comparisons between what is described by "is proud of his
beautiful house" and "is proud of his beautiful body." Likewise, the theory
is blind to similarities in what is described by "is proud of his new house"
and "is ashamed of his new house" because each describes a "unitary phenomenon." If one gives up the idea of a directed emotion as a "unitary
phenomenon," it is possible to reconcile the hypothesis that "is proud of
his beautiful house" describes a property of its subject, with the desire not
to lose the information of its structural components. This would require a
theory that offers a way of matching the complex structure of the complete
emotion predicate to a complex emotional state of the individual. This
possibility is in principle not admitted by Solomon.[45]

Finally, Solomon's way of looking at intentionality of emotion is not unlike accounts of perception that focus on perceptual experience, dismissing
its relational aspect entirely. Perceptual experience might indeed be worth
looking at, but for many this does not exhaust our concept of perception.
Likewise, if one agrees with Solomon's way of carving up intentionality,
one forfeits the picture of object directedness in its relational form. Moreover, Solomon gives us no way of reintroducing the world into the picture,
because these emotional states are opaque, unanalyzable into the appropriate components. We must forfeit the idea that Frank's loving Susan
has anything to do with Susan. Perhaps a compromise is possible whereby
intentionality would refer to the experiential correlate of an object-directed
emotion, but there might still be an independent item that is the emotion's
object. Wilson tries to maintain both these aspects of directedness.

4. Arnold

Arnold is one of the few representatives of the psychological tradition who
makes reference to emotion's object directedness. For the rest there appears
to be a conspiracy of silence on the topic. Even so, this occurs only in
Arnold's early work.[46] I make a note of her remarks on the objects of
emotion as they illustrate the confusion that arises if one adopts a naive
causal picture of object directedness. Wilson, on the contrary, carefully

---

[45] For excellent discussion of these issues in the context of other cognitive
attitudes, see J. Barwise and J. Perry, *Situations and Attitudes*.

[46] M. B. Arnold, *Emotion and Personality*, vol. I.

delimits the domain of his causal analysis thereby avoiding some of the usual pitfalls.

Arnold points out that an episode of an emotion involves not only a subject experiencing the emotion but, in addition, the emotion's object. She initially identifies the object to be "someone or something that occasions the experience" and the item or situation to which emotion carries a reference.[47] She adds, further:

> The object or situation may be actually present, as in the reunion of lovers after long absence. It may be in the past, as a remembered injury done to a friend. It may be the anticipation of some future event, as an impending automobile collision. Emotion may even be aroused by something merely imagined, as the possible loss of a job, or winning the Grand Prize in the Irish Sweep.

The problem of explicating directedness to future and imagined events is a recurrent one. It is the constant thorn in the side of a naive causal analysis. One cannot assert that the object of emotion is that which occasions or arouses it and at the same time allow the object to be a future or imagined event. Perhaps Arnold could avoid these problems by making more of the notion of the object of emotion being something that an emotion carries reference to. Unfortunately, she does not develop this idea any further. A causal analysis must be reconciled with the intuition that in many cases emotions appear to be directed to objects that are outside the causal order. Wilson's approach offers one way of dealing with this problem.

5. Wilson

Wilson recognizes the vagueness and ambiguity in most discussions of emotion's object directedness.[48] He attributes this to the fact that the term "object of emotion" is applied in far too unrestricted a domain. The first step Wilson takes toward a theory of object directedness is a careful delimitation of the cases that fall within his domain of inquiry. He wishes to restrict the term "object directedness" to these cases. The situations

---

[47] Both characterizations occur in *Emotion and Personality* vol. I, p. 170.

[48] All references to Wilson are from J. R. S. Wilson, *Emotion and Object*, 1972.

that interest him include as components an individual having an emotion and an item that exists independently of the individual, such that the item and the emotion stand in a special sort of relation to one another—one in which the individual is "emotionally concerned with the item."[49] An emotion is object directed if there is an item in the world that stands in this relation to it. Wilson uses the generic term "item in the world" to cover individuals, events, actions, states, and properties. Wilson's goal is to come to an understanding of the relation between an emotion and its object to discover what must be true about the emotion, about the item, and about their mutual interaction in order for the item to be the emotion's object.[50]

Wilson cuts out a large chunk of what others have considered central cases of object-directed emotions. He notes two such categories. One is the category of "malfounded emotions." This includes cases of emotions in which the subject believes the emotion to be directed but for which no corresponding relatum exists, for example, through mistaken identity. The other is the category of "intentional emotions." He includes here cases in which the emotion is described by a sentence containing the emotion verb followed by a propositional clause, as "He is angry that he was overlooked for the prize." Future-directed emotions such as dread and fear represent another type of intentional but non-object-directed emotion. Presumably Wilson would want to exclude the cases Arnold depicts as ones in which the object is merely imagined.

Hume's approach to the problem of the analysis of object-directed emotions is limited in scope and is fairly concrete. Following Hume, the trend has been toward greater complexity and abstraction. Against this backdrop, Wilson's approach smacks of the reactionary. He wants to put relationality back into the emotion-object relation and wants "objects" to be objects. Wilson preserves Hume's picture in taking a concrete particular to be the object of a directed emotion. In this he diverges from Rorty. The emotion's object stands in a causal relation to the emotion. Wilson takes the metaphysical question to be the primary one. He examines the nature of the emotion-object relation first and then considers the utterances that

---

49 *Ibid.*, p. 74.

50 Wilson notes that, strictly speaking, the relation is not an emotion-object relation but is actually a relation between the object and the person having the emotion, or even the person's having the emotion. For greater convenience, we continue to use the label "emotion-object relation."

supposedly report these relations. This contrasts with Kenny and Thalberg, who use structural features of language to inform us of emotion's object directedness.

Wilson attempts to formulate conditions on the emotion-object relation that are both necessary and sufficient. The situations that are the focus of Wilson's examination are comprised of an emotion e, an item in the world o, and a relation R between the two in virtue of which the item is the object of the emotion. Wilson proposes conditions that are necessary and sufficient for the situation $e \; R \; o$. He comes up with a two-condition analysis. He characterizes it as a causal analysis of object directedness because one of the conditions stipulates that the object, the item in the world, be causally related to the emotion. Before outlining Wilson's formulation and his defense of these conditions, I introduce certain of the key terms and notions that Wilson makes use of.

Wilson adopts Davidson's refinement of the Humean notion of causation. He emphasizes three tenets in particular: (i) Properly speaking, the relation of cause to effect holds between events only; (ii) events related as cause to effect are thus related by virtue of their being subsumable under a causal law; and (iii) mental events may enter into cause-effect relations.

Though the relation between an emotion and its object is a causal one, it may not be the relation between effect and cause. In weakening certain of the conditions on the relation between an effect to its cause, Wilson derives the notion of *causal relatedness*, and it is this weaker relation that underlies the emotion-object relation. There is a greater range of possibilities in the types of items that may be causally related. An individual is causally related to a given event if the individual is an agent in the event that causes it; for example, a murderer is causally related to the murder. The acted upon individual is also a causal relatum; therefore, the murderer bears a causal relation to the victim, a tailor to the shirt she mends, and so forth. Causal relata need not be contiguous. The death of the old lady in the nursery rhyme is causally related to her swallowing the fly, despite the lengthy sequence of intervening events. Wilson unfortunately provides no further description of the causal relation said to partially comprise the emotion-object relation.

I have already suggested that the objects of emotion are items in the world, noting the categories that this covers. Wilson offers the following rough characterization of the second relatum in the emotion-object relation—the emotion itself. An emotion, or rather an instance of an emotion, is an event occurring within a determinate space-time location, involving an individual's occurrent experiential state. It is a complex response, an agglomeration of mental and possibly even physical reactions. Feeling features prominently among these for almost all types of emotions. In addition to feelings, there are cognitive components, alterations in patterns of attention and thought. Further, the emotion might involve impulses or desires to act in certain ways. Impulses feature importantly in Wilson's analysis of object directedness. They are different from desires in that they are 'real-time' mental events, undeliberated and spontaneous. In contrast, desires are dispositional in nature and deliberate. A desire is a component of an emotion (and not its cause or consequence) only if the desire is directed to the object and not to the attainment of some ulterior goal. If one pities another individual, a desire to help the individual is partially constitutive of one's pity only if helping the person is seen as an end in itself and not as a means of achieving an ulterior goal, such as earning the admiration of onlookers. Similarly, gratitude frequently involves a desire to repay one's helper; anger, a desire to harm one's antagonist.

The Causal Condition.   The causal condition requires that the emotion stand in a causal relation to its object. This is broken down into two stages. First, it is necessary that the emotion be caused by the subject's *attending* to the object. "Attending to" is a generic label for a range of acts of mental apprehension including perceiving, thinking about, learning of, knowing, and remembering. Notice that this does not yet assure the causal connection between the emotion and its object but only between the emotion and a mental act of apprehension. The link is completed by finding the appropriate tie between the item in the world and the act of mental apprehension that is an apprehension of that item. This is the second stage. As we might have expected, Wilson proposes a further causal link between the act of apprehension and the object. He backs this up in the case of perception by citing Grice's version of a causal analysis of perception. He offers his own suggestions for a causal analysis of "thinking about." It would involve too great a digression here to look further at Wilson's very interesting attempt. He might also have noted that elsewhere a causal analysis of memory has been offered.[51]

Consider the working of the causal condition in the following example: In order to say that the object of one's disgust is a burst sewage pipe, it must be the case that one's apprehension of the burst pipe causes one's

---

[51] C. B. Martin and M. Deutcher, "Remembering," *Philosophical Review*, 1966.

disgust. In this case, let us say that one sees and smells the burst pipe. The burst pipe is causally related to one's disgust by being causally responsible for one's seeing and smelling it. This is implied by a causal theory of perception. Apprehending the burst pipe, in turn, causes the experience of disgust.

Wilson draws a parallel between his causal analysis of the emotion-object relation and a causal analysis of "object of perception." As in perception, the causal condition is not a sufficient one since many events, states, individuals, and properties are related causally to the emotion but are not the emotion's object. It is not difficult to construct cases demonstrating the insufficiency of the causal condition. For example, my hearing the gears of my car grinding is a causal antecedent of my anger. The gears grinding is a sign that the mechanic to whom I recently paid three hundred dollars has failed to repair the clutch properly. I want to be able to say that the negligent mechanic is the object of my anger and not the grinding gears, even though the latter satisfies the causal condition. Wilson gives the example of a man who becomes sad on listening to the piece of music he heard the night before his wife died. It is not the music's playing that is the emotion's object, despite the fact that hearing it causes the man's sadness. It is the wife's dying that is the object of the man's emotion.

Wilson offers a second condition that selects from all the causal relata the one that is the emotion's object. It seems there are two ways an additional condition could function. One is that, given the causal sequence leading to the event in question, the condition serves to circumscribe a 'slot' in the sequence. Whatever fills this slot is the targeted item. Causal theories of perception adopt this strategy in selecting the object of perception from other causal relata. Wilson hints that this is his strategy but, in fact, appears to follow a different one. According that one, one distinguishes the target from the other causal relata by virtue of an additional relation that *it* bears to the emotion, irrespective of its position in the causal sequence.

Wilson offers an additional constraint on objects that he describes as the requirement that the emotion be "in some sense relevant or appropriate to, or determined in its nature by" its object.[52] I use the phrases "relevance condition" and "*R*-condition" to refer to this constraint. In most of what follows in this section, I try to make sense of the relevance condition, seeing whether together with the causal condition it converges on the objects

---

[52] Wilson, *op. cit.*, p. 82.

of emotion. In other words, I test whether Wilson has indeed provided necessary and sufficient conditions for the relation of object to emotion.[53]

The Relevance Condition.   Wilson gives independent accounts of the relevance condition for the cases in which the item in question is an event and those in which it is an individual. In explicating the condition, I maintain this separation because the two accounts are different from each other in important ways. Wilson limits his discussion of the *R*-condition to these two categories. I begin by considering the case of events.

In a succinct statement of the additional requirement Wilson writes, "The emotion must be relevant or appropriate to the event. That is, the nature of the emotion must be determined by features of the event itself."[54] A brief look at this passage should suffice to draw attention to one of the problems with Wilson's condition, that is, the problem of discovering what precisely it is. In the first place, the terms he uses in the statement are not self-explanatory and do not pick out properties one would normally associate with emotions. This problem is exacerbated by the following fact: Wilson asserts that the emotion is relevant to its object. In explicating this requirement he offers two further characterizations, that the emotion be appropriate to its object and that its nature be determined by the object. Evidently, in the passage above, it appears that Wilson intends the two characterizations to be alternative ways of converging on just one condition. I contend that this is not so. I argue that his description of the condition involves at least two distinct possibilities. I claim, further, that neither of the versions of Wilson's R-condition for events successfully completes the analysis of the emotion-object relation.

In showing that the *R*-condition is not satisfied in the case of the man listening to the music, Wilson focuses on the phrase "the nature of the emotion must be determined by features of the event itself." In this case, the man's sadness must be determined by features of the music itself. Wilson explains this requirement further by contrasting the case in which an emotional reaction is determined by "internal features" of an item with the case in which the reaction is determined by features that are merely accidental to it. The case of the man's sadness does not illustrate an emotion-object relation because his emotional response to the music is determined by its

---

[53] I should stress that I remain within the constraints of Wilson's scope delimitations.

[54] *Ibid.*, p. 85.

accidental association with the true object of the man's sadness, his wife's death. With no guidance from Wilson, it seems reasonable to suppose that the association of the music with the emotional reaction is accidental because only by dint of its past spatiotemporal contiguity with the death episode does it effect the emotional reaction. This supposition makes available a fairly precise method for identifying at least some of those cases in which an event brings about an emotional reaction but fails to do so by virtue of its internal features.

I concur with Wilson in judging that the music is not the object of the man's sadness. Nevertheless, I find questionable his principled means of arriving at this judgment. We see that the version of the relevance condition under discussion is an insufficient supplement to the causal condition because there is a class of cases in which the condition is satisfied but that do not constitute cases of emotion-object relations. In other words, there are cases in which internal features of an event determine the nature of the emotional reaction to the event, but the event is not the object of the emotion. Consider the following situation. One is listening to someone recount stories about Nazi concentration camps. This evokes a feeling of horror and disgust. The person's telling about the camps[55] is causally responsible for one's emotional reaction. One's emotional reaction is determined by internal features of the event: the features of the utterance by virtue of which it acquires its meaning. Yet I judge that the camps themselves are the objects of one's emotion and not the utterance. The utterance evokes the emotional response by referring to historical events; however, it is by no means accidental that it does so.

Further, cases of this type call into question the contrast Wilson draws between "determined by internal features" and "determined by mere accidental association." One judges the music to be the object of the man's emotional response only if "the nature of his response is determined by features of the music itself, rather than by association with something else."[56] This fails to adjudicate correctly in the case of utterances because utterances evoke emotional reactions *because* of their systematic association with other events—namely, what they refer to. Wilson contrasts responses elicited because of the accidental association of their stimuli with another event, with responses elicited by virtue of "internal features" of the stim-

---

[55] That's the utterance, where utterance is taken to be a certain course of events, along the lines posited in situation semantics.

[56] *Ibid.*, p. 83.

ulus. These associations are not accidental but are made by virtue of internal features of the utterance. The statement quoted above is rendered paradoxical in light of these examples. They show that the straightforward interpretation of "internal features of the object" that contrasts these with features merely accidental to it, which in turn are seen to be features the item acquires by dint of its spatial and temporal location, is not sufficient to ground the *R*-condition. But since Wilson offers no other way of interpreting this version of the *R*-condition, it must be rejected.

I turn now to a second characterization used in the *R*-condition, shifting focus from the requirement that the nature of the emotion be determined by features of the object itself to the requirement that it be *appropriate* to the object. I will call this the "second version" of the *R*-condition. Wilson draws on an analogy with action. One judges an action appropriate to a situation to the extent that the action is consistent with the agent's goals or furthers his ends in some way. Wilson contends that an emotion may also be judged appropriate or inappropriate. The judgment is not made on the basis of the emotion's service to an agent's ends. It is based on how well the emotion fits with an intuitive principle according to which one sees certain types of emotional responses as 'right' for certain occasions and not for others. For example, it is right to experience fear in the face of danger, sympathy over someone else's tribulations, and mirth on hearing a good joke. This idea of appropriateness ties in with appropriateness of an action in that, generally speaking, both suggest a measure of the success of the activity against some valued standard. Wilson stipulates further that it makes sense to judge an instance of an emotion or action appropriate or inappropriate only if there is sufficient variability in other instances of the same type across individuals and locations. If a response, an action or emotion, is stereotypically evoked in a certain situation, then "there is no room for saying that one effect is more appropriate than another."[57]

The notion of appropriateness is at best a red herring. It neither merges with the conception of relevance discussed above nor offers a superior way of capturing the notion of object directedness. It is not clear why Wilson requires variability in the response to a certain stimulus as a prerequisite for judging any of these appropriate to it. Feeling terror on facing a snarling lion in the open bush is probably as uniform a response across individuals as one could find. According to the ideas of most, the response is certainly appropriate to the stimulus. Setting this point aside, I take

---

[57]   Ibid., p. 82.

up the question of the place of appropriateness in the relevance condition. Consider another example. A woman feels jealous on seeing her husband talking to another woman at a party. In this case, the emotional response is determined by internal features of the eliciting situation. Yet one could argue persuasively that the response is inappropriate to it. In this case, the first version is successful in identifying the emotion's object; her husband's talking to another woman at the party is the object of the woman's jealousy. Appropriateness is, in fact, not even a necessary condition on object directedness, for consider the feeling of disgust elicited on seeing someone torture an animal. This is surely the *right* response to the situation. If, however, the response is elicited because one finds the blood unsightly, the disgust is not directed to the torturing per se. In other words, the response is appropriate to the torturing but we would not say that the torturing is the object of disgust.

In the discussion above, I have attempted to highlight two causes for dissatisfaction with Wilson's relevance condition. One is that Wilson's description of the condition allows for several possible interpretations. A more serious problem is that it fails to capture the emotion-object relation so that even when the relevance and causal conditions are combined they do not yield necessary and sufficient conditions on the emotion-object relation. I think that, in fact, the condition more or less systematically spotlights a quite different, also noteworthy, causal antecedent. It happens not to be the one we want.

Causal relatedness is a weak causal notion. It binds an event with causal factors that do not necessarily qualify for the title "the cause." In the often cited example of a match lighting on being struck, the striking is the event's cause, while factors like sufficient oxygen's being present and the match's being dry are identified as enabling conditions. Wilson's causal relatedness covers these types of causal factors as well as *the* cause. Without going too deeply into the question of how one distinguishes mere causal relata from causes, I offer one suggestion, repeating a comment from the section on Hume. We recognize a phenomenon to be the cause of an event if, ceteris paribus, the phenomenon is sufficient to bring the event about. This sufficiency explains why causes are so often cited in explanations of an event's occurrence. If asked to explain the match's lighting, one cites the fact that it was struck, since ceteris paribus this is a sufficient condition for the lighting to occur.

My suggestion is that the relevance condition functions to select from among the causal relata the one that has significant explanatory power and not the emotion's object. Frequently, this will be *the* cause. Recall Wilson's example of the man saddened on hearing a piece of music. The music is not the object of the man's sadness because it elicits the emotion by its accidental association with his wife's death. Think of a different example now: a man listening to a sad piece of music, perhaps a particularly moving rendition of "Greensleeves." Certain features are associated with the evocative power of this piece—its minor key, its tempo, and so forth. Whatever they are, one would agree that insofar as the emotion is elicited by this piece of music, it is elicited by dint of internal features of the music.[58] The relevance condition is satisfied by this case. However, whereas one might *explain* the man's emotional state by citing the playing of "Greensleeves," one hardly wants to classify the music as the object of the emotion. My suggestion sheds light on another of the examples. Recall the listener horrified on hearing stories about Nazi concentration camps. It is plausible to suggest that the nature of the emotional response is determined by internal features of the utterance because there is a systematic connection between the utterance, the emotion, and the event it describes. One assumes that the utterance is an assertion by someone whom the listener trusts and involves expressions with a certain meaning. The systematic ties ground the explanatory relevance of the utterance to the emotion. (In fact, the same goes for the event and the emotion.) If I were to ask *why* the individual displayed the emotions of horror and disgust, a reasonable reply would be to explain that he had *been informed* about the Nazi camps. In other words, the *R*-condition succeeds in selecting an explanatorily relevant factor.

My proposal is tentative in that I do not draw on a precise notion of an "explanatorily relevant factor." Nor am I suggesting that Wilson's *R*-condition constitutes a theory of explanation of emotion. I merely suggest that the *R*-condition appears directed more to this notion than to that of 'objecthood'. I have attempted to illustrate with the music examples that the two notions are distinct.

I now turn to the relevance condition for individuals. Taking *A* to be the individual having the emotion and *B* another individual (it is possible that *A* and *B* are the same) Wilson expresses the condition as follows:

> *A*'s emotion will only have *B* as its object if it is relevant to *B* in some way further to being caused by attention to *B*. The nature of

---

[58] Of course, there is also the possibility that the music is associated with sad memories, in which case the sadness is presumably overdetermined.

A's emotion must be determined by features of B himself, or perhaps better, by features which A attributes to B himself.[59]

Wilson introduces a new dimension in interpreting the condition for individuals; he requires that the emotion be "specifically determined in its nature by the item."[60] The new condition has two components: First, as in the case of events, the type of the emotion is determined by the nature of the item and not by virtue of the item's accidental association with something else; and second, the emotion must be "specific" to the item. The second component dominates Wilson's conception of the R-condition as it applies to individuals. I limit my discussion to it.

Wilson uses the notion of specificity to capture a certain relation between a response and its stimulus. A response is specific to a stimulus if it varies systematically with variation in the stimulus. One needs to introduce a counterfactual conditional in order to spell out this relation as it applies to instances of stimuli and responses.[61] For a particular stimulus-response pair, the response is specific to its stimulus if, were it the case that the stimulus had been of a different type, the response would have been different. Another way of describing this situation is by saying that the response is highly sensitive to a certain range of variations in the stimulus. Given that a response is sensitive to certain variations in stimulus, if one were to monitor the response very closely one would acquire information in this indirect way about the nature of the stimulus. Where the response is an emotion, the new R-condition requires that there be systematic covariation between features of individuals eliciting the emotion and features of the emotion itself; the emotion is sensitive to its object.

Before I discuss its application to emotion, I remark on one serious omission in Wilson's account of specificity. He fails to fill one important parameter. Whether or not one judges a certain pair of events to be specific to each other will depend on how fine grained one expects the systematic covariation to be. One might teach a pigeon to peck on a key in response to the presentation of a slide in which water is depicted. The pigeon's pecking varies *systematically* with the nature of the stimuli but not on a very fine grain. A child responding to the same slides with verbal descriptions of them exhibits a response that varies systematically but is sensitive to a

---

[59] *Ibid.* p. 33.

[60] *Ibid.*, p. 90

[61] This fact is not explicitly recognized by Wilson.

greater number of distinct features of the stimulus. In the limiting case, a response would be specific *up to the individual*, by which I mean that the response is sensitive to any change in identity of the stimulus. Wilson does not address this issue directly and equivocates over the extent of the covariation between object and emotion that his theory requires. At times, he demands specificity up to the individual. Yet, in discussing intentional emotions that do not have objects, he relies on the fact that emotional responses are specific only up to the type of an individual that is causally related to the emotion. I try to avoid this issue in the discussion that follows.

The relevance condition for individuals must satisfy two queries. First, given the specificity requirement and what we know about Wilson's conception of emotion, does the latter support the former? Second, assuming it is possible to show that emotions are capable of varying systematically with variation in certain individuals as stimuli, does this condition converge on the emotion-object relation? I begin with the first.

Impulse or desire to act is the key component of emotion responsible for the possibility of covariation of an emotional response with certain stimuli. According to Wilson, many emotions involve impulses to act. To bolster his hypothesis that impulse is the key factor, Wilson makes the dubious observation that emotions that involve impulses, including fear, anger, hatred, pity, and envy, are typically those that have individuals as their objects. Wilson explains the way impulses acquire specificity beginning with the actions that the impulses are behind. He notes that actions are frequently object directed: One flees a snarling dog, gives money to a decrepit beggar, embraces one's child. Wilson takes the directedness one stage backward, or inward, using the characteristics of the action-object relation as a means of individuating the impulse to action. An impulse precedes an action and is a psychological phenomenon. Presumably, there are impulses that are not followed by their matching actions but will be directed to a certain object. Wilson provides no account of the impulse-object relation nor does he explain the assumption that impulses are directed to the same objects as are the subsequent actions and that this partially determines their identity. Nevertheless, he relies on this assumption in asserting that the impulse to embrace one's child is a different type of mental act from the impulse to flee the snarling dog and is also different from the impulse to embrace one's mother. In the following passage, Wilson explains the connection of this fact to the emotion-object relation:

When an emotion arouses fear, on the other hand, the response is specific to the object. Thus if there are behavioral tendencies involved, these relate to the particular object in question—when perception of A causes fear, the behavioral impulse involved is, let us suppose, to escape from A, when perception of B causes fear, it is to escape from B, and so on.[62]

There is a strong matching between an impulse to behave and the behavior. Wilson assumes, moreover, that the nature of the impulse is also partially determined by the identity of the object of action. I say "identity" and not "type" since Wilson in the above passage seems to suppose that the impulse to escape from A is dissimilar from the impulse to escape from B simply on the grounds that A and B are distinct individuals.

This is an extremely strong claim about the intentionality or directedness of an impulse. If it could be successfully argued for, it would certainly provide grounds for the claim that an emotion involving an impulse to behave varies systematically with variations in the stimulus individual. It is a strong claim, for it is equivalent to asserting that impulses are specific to the objects of behavior, up to identity of the individual. A vigilant Humean would argue that this is impossible since it implies a necessary connection between distinct items in the world. Aside from this, I have the following qualm about Wilson's claim: How is it possible for an impulse to bear the stamp of identity of the individual that is its object if the action itself does not? Consider the two actions, escaping from A and escaping from B, A and B distinct. The difference between these two actions is found in the distinct relational characteristics of these events and not in the nature of the *activity* involved in each. By this I mean that there are no differences in the purely behavioral features of the two cases of escaping (i.e., if one focuses on features of the escaping agents) accountable to the fact that in the one case the agent is escaping from A and in the other from B. One may describe this fact using Wilson's terminology by noting that the activity of escaping is not specific to the individual one is escaping from. I conclude that it is not possible for an *impulse* to be specific to the individual on the grounds that it is not possible in the case of action. Further, there is no way of accounting for the directedness or intentionality of impulses which will serve the demands placed on impulses that Wilson places on them.

---

[62] *Ibid.* p. 37.

I conclude this section on Wilson by going over some of the main issues raised in the discussion above, closing with a general appraisal of Wilson's position.

Wilson presupposes as a condition of object directedness the requirement that an object-directed emotion bear a special sort of relation to an item in the world existing independently of the emoting subject. He gives a causal analysis of the emotion-object relation offering two necessary and jointly sufficient conditions on this relation. First, a causal condition: An item is the object of an emotion only if it is causally related to the emotion. This is weaker than the requirement that the object be the emotion's cause. The causal condition is obviously not a sufficient one. Wilson imposes the further condition that the emotion be relevant to the item. The relevance-condition (as I called it) selects from among an emotion's causal relata the item that is its object. Wilson offers separate accounts of relevance as it applies to events and individuals. For an emotion to be relevant to an event its type must be determined by internal features of the event. He contrasts these cases with ones in which the event and emotion are causally related to one another by mere accidental association. An emotion is relevant to an individual who is causally related to it if the emotion is specific to the individual. An emotion is specific to an individual if it is systematically linked to that individual. This occurs when one of the constituents of an emotion is an impulse to behave directed toward that individual.

Wilson's theory, according to the conditions of Chapter 1, is clearly relational. It incorporates neither a linguistic condition nor a condition explicitly requiring the explanatory relevance of the object. If, however, one accepts my interpretation of his R-condition, Wilson's theory converges precisely on factors that are explanatorily relevant to the emotion. The intentional-state condition brings out an interesting feature of Wilson's approach: his attempt to separate object directedness from intentionality. Directed emotions are instances of intentional states; but this is only one half of the picture. If the item in the world does not exist, standing in the appropriate relation to an intentional emotional state, the emotion is not object directed.

Even if one supports the spirit of Wilson's enterprise—to provide a causal analysis of the emotion-object relation—one must recognize that the relevance condition fails to fulfill its stated function. In the case of events, the condition boils down to a demand for a lawlike connection between emotion and object. In the case of individuals, the requirement of systematic covariation between features of the object with features of the emotion strongly suggest a demand for a lawlike connection. The problem with this is that, though the condition succeeds in selecting an item that has a special bearing on the emotion, it fails to capture our intuitive notion of object directedness.

The idea that the object of emotion is the individual toward which an impulse is directed is more promising in its ability to capture the intuitively based judgments of object directedness but has its own problem. Wilson's analysis of the emotion-object relation, in this context, amounts to locating it at a different mental phenomenon, one that is a component of the emotion itself. He ends up with this: An individual *o* is the object of an emotion *e*, if and only if *o* is causally related to *e* and *e* involves an impulse to behave that has *o* as its object. Judging from what Wilson says in the passage below, it appears that he considers his analysis to have achieved a more complete reduction of the emotion-object relation:

> In this way the relation between an emotion and its object is not at all mysterious but reduces to a familiar and comprehensible one. But to say that an item is the object of an emotion is not just to say that it is its cause. The notion of an object is a more specific notion.[63]

I think this shows that Wilson misconstrues the power of his analysis. Perhaps because he does not see the importance of the impulse-object relation for his analysis, Wilson says very little about it. Aside from the fact that Wilson seems not to fulfill his stated reduction, his technical use of the notion of an impulse diverges from normal usage. This is a problem for his analysis because, if the analysis of something as complex as emotion's object directedness is to be given in terms of the directedness of another mental phenomenon, little is achieved if the latter is an ill-defined theoretical phenomenon. And if we are to believe Ryle, "Impulses, described as feelings which impel actions, are para-mechanical myths."[64] My own analysis of an analogue of the emotion-object relation, given in the concluding chapter, bears some resemblance to Wilson's. The analysis is not offered as a complete reduction of emotion's intentionality in terms of nonintentional phenomena, but the components of the analysis are limited to familiar elements of the mental.

---

[63] *Ibid.*, p. 39.

[64] Ryle, G., *The Concept of Mind*, pp. 114–115.

Chapter 3

Disbanding the Project

1. The Many Faces of Object Directedness

To give the reader an intuitive idea of what object directedness is, I generated a set of cases that would qualify as typical cases of emotions that have objects. I described these cases in Chaptert 1 in the list of statements, 1–9. I intended the sample to reflect the wide range of types of emotions with objects and the variation in structure of the statements themselves that may be used to indicate object directedness. To make precise the notion of object directedness, one asks what must be true about an episode involving emotion, that is what conditions must be satisfied by an instance of emotion in order that it be judged an object directed emotion. Any attempt to analyze object directedness is then evaluated against the intuitively generated set of cases.

The task is a straightforward one of providing a conceptual theory, but it has met with peculiarly little success. It remains impossible to articulate principles that underlie the concept of object directedness of emotion. The attempts to analyze object directedness outlined in Chapter 2 were shown to be seriously flawed. Another notable feature of the selection is their diversity. Seen as a succession of theories directed to a common goal, they display surprisingly little overlap and seem to disagree with one another on fundamental issues. This much should be evident from the descriptions of views presented in the preceding chapter. In this chapter, I turn my attention to the question of *why* it has proved so difficult to come up with principles that provide a core to the understanding of object directedness— ones that would appeal to a majority of those investigating the issue.

I argue that the problems faced by several views on object directedness and the failure to agree on a core set of underlying principles are symptoms of a deeper problem. The intuitive beginnings of the notion of object directedness are unsound. The set of cases that are supposedly generated by the intuitive notion do not form an adequate basis for a theory because they do not emerge from a natural category. The spectrum of cases that currently ground the supposed notion of object directedness is too wide to be captured by a reasonable notion. The diversity of the set of cases creates a problem for those who hold the mistaken belief that there *is* a single concept covering the entire class of cases, one for which they must provide a set of conditions.

I offer an alternative perspective on the issue, one that I believe will have a progressive effect on the study of emotion and its object directedness. My first recommendation is that we abandon the notion "object directedness"—abandon it because it has no natural existence. Let me put the recommendation a bit more conservatively: We must disband object directedness—take it apart. The statements 1–9 describe examples of several important and interesting features of emotion, each of which deserves attention. The class of currently acknowledged cases of object-directed emotions should be dissected into its more unified clusters. This recommendation is not disconnected from the tradition of attempts to analyze object directedness. Rather, it comes from a careful examination of what is at the bottom of the consistent failure to produce a convincing one. If one looks closely at the source of some of the disagreements among theories of object directedness, one finds that the dissection of the notion is already taking place but is unacknowledged. The disagreements are not genuine but stem from differences in the implicit foci of distinct theories.

In the first part of this chapter, I examine some of the persistent points of disagreement among the views outlined in Chapter 2. These points do not provide the means—as is usual in the evaluation of competing theories—for comparing and choosing between theories but draw attention to the fact that some of these theories are incommensurable. I argue that in specifying conditions on object directedness each theory picks a cluster out of the larger set of cases, one for which the theory is especially fitting. The theory does not apply to the entire class because the conditions preserve features that are not universal to the class. Incommensurability results when distinct theories happen to be directed to distinct clusters of cases. In the second part of the chapter, I suggest a way to rework the ground previously covered by the notion of object directedness. I enumerate and offer brief descriptions of several of its distinct components, some of which are suggested by the four conditions of Chapter 1.

2. Uncovering the Differences

Looked at superficially, Wilson's and Kenny's views are in direct conflict. Wilson offers a causal analysis of the emotion-object relation. Kenny claims that the connection between emotion and object is noncontingent, arguing that a causal analysis of object directedness is not possible. Wilson, whose view postdates Kenny's by some ten years, goes to a lot of trouble to interpret and eventually to discredit Kenny's position. Yet the disagreement is actually spurious, since, in explicating object directedness in terms of a relation between emotions and items in the world, Wilson theorizes about a different phenomenon from the one about which Kenny makes his stipulations. The fact that Wilson succeeds in showing that the noncontingency thesis does not apply in a scenario in which the object of emotion is an independent concrete particular holds no sway for a supporter of Kenny's position. This person ignores Wilson's comments, saying they are not applicable to the *real* question of object directedness. The result is a standoff, the two parties realizing that their conflicting views are directed toward distinct territories. Their actual disagreement is not over whether the connection is contingent or not, causal or not, but over what the units of investigation are, where in the world one looks for object-directed emotions.

Let us take a look at Kenny's perspective on the situation and his argument against the possibility that objects are causal precursors of emotions. His argument is directed against a causal analysis but in fact takes on one of the hypotheses that a causal analysis presupposes. I briefly summarize it as follows: A causal analysis is possible only if an emotion's object is a permissible link in the causal order. Take the simple case of a theory in which the object of an emotion is its cause. The theory would be ridiculous if the objects of one's theory were not of the type capable of causing, or of standing in a causal relation to something. Taking into consideration the emotions described later in this section in the examples 1–9 of David's dread, John's fear, and June's jealousy, directed toward future events, merely possible events, and events only imagined in the mind of the subject, the ridiculous is realized. These examples indicate objects of emotion that have no place in the causal order. A causal analysis is thereby precluded.

Kenny considers one rather ad hoc solution to his challenge: The objects of emotion are mental images or mental representations. The cognitive state causes an emotion. This avoids the problem caused by future-looking emotions and ones directed to possible occurrences. Magda Arnold is impressed by the problem and suggests a solution along these lines. In the previous chapter, I indicated the confusion in her view that results from both moves. Kenny rejects the proposed solution, saying that mental images or representations are not the objects of emotion because people do not fear and dread ideas or mental representations-they fear and dread real things.

I find Kenny's rejoinder unconvincing because it is inconsistent with the view of object directedness that he supports. After all, Kenny goes to great lengths to repudiate a causal analysis in order to strengthen his own nonrelational account of the noncontingent connection between emotion and object. Therefore, according to Kenny, there actually is not any *thing* that is the object of emotion. Kenny's rejoinder is effective only if one takes the object to be an independent item toward which the emotion is directed. Since his own theory does not incorporate this view, Kenny's rejoinder is ultimately insupportable. If one gives up the idea of an object as the emotion's focal point, Kenny has no argument that chooses his picture over one that presents ideas or mental representations as the objects of emotion.

Even if one is not convinced by Kenny's rejoinder to the move to internalize, his original argument against a causal analysis appears to be an extremely powerful one. Yet if one attends carefully to its presuppositions, its force is lost on all but the already converted. One must share Kenny's conviction in the decisive role of linguistic expression in forming one's judgments on the intentional status of an emotion *as well as* his determination to treat these cases uniformly within his theory. The entire discussion of the two preceding paragraphs could be short-circuited by one who is convinced by the picture of extended, independently existing objects of emotion. One simply challenges Kenny's assumption that every complex emotion sentence of the type he specifies describes an object-directed emotion. This is precisely what was accomplished in Wilson's scope demarcation.

It is reasonable to expect a proponent of a theory of object directedness to be able to answer the question "What are the objects of emotion?" Are they concrete particulars or abstractions? Do they exist independently of the subject or are they figments of the imagination? This raises another disputable issue. Consider the diverse answers given to this question. Hume's is very precise in that he specifies for each type of emotion he discusses the exact type of its object. The self is the object of pride and humility, another individual is the object of love and hatred, and so on. There are English sentences that describe these relations, ones like "He is proud of himself" and "Jim loves Martha." But not every statement with a structure similar to these describes an emotion-object relation. Significantly, "He is proud of his new house" and "She hates his aggressive manner" do not.

Wilson's objects are also extended items in the world standing in a particular relation to some individual's emotional experience. His analysis of object directedness is motivated by metaphysical concerns, and only in a limited spectrum of cases is this reflected in the way we speak about emotions. "Frank loves Susan" and "Hannah is angry that she was not invited" describe emotion-object relations; "David dreads meeting his ex-wife" does not.

The objects of emotions are intentional objects, according to Rorty. She appears to contradict the positions of both Hume and Wilson in calling it a mistake to think that emotion's objects are extended items in the world. After all, one may resent someone for qualities they do not actually possess, grow fond of someone qua holder of a title or social position, or be angry at the wrong person for making a dent in one's new automobile. Rorty posits the existence of intentional objects having just the properties that the individual attributes to them. These are not extended items because we are able to discriminate in far greater detail the intentional component of an emotion than is possible for extended objects.

A supporter of either Kenny's or Solomon's positions judges "What are the objects of emotion?" an improper question since both hold to a view that denies relationality. There *is* no object of emotion. Object directedness is a feature that an emotion has in virtue of the sentences we may use to describe it. It is just as well that Kenny averts the search for the appropriate ontological category, given the range of cases it would have to satisfy. Here are some examples:

1. Frank loves Susan.
2. Paul regrets having refused to invest in Apple Computers.
3. David is dreading seeing his ex-wife.
4. John fears a nuclear war.
5. Ann is jealous because she thinks the writer is her husband's lover.
6. Phoebe is proud to be an American.
7. Hannah is angry that she was not invited to the party.
8. Hannah is angry at Rhoda for not inviting her to the party.

Compare the answers provided by Wilson, Rorty, and Kenny to the "what is" question. (Hume's and Solomon's answers are not sufficiently unique to warrant separate discussion.) Despite the appearance of conflict among them, this is not a simple case of different judgments made about a common set of phenomena. It is not the case that they all point to the same phenomenon, Wilson claiming it to be concrete, Rorty claiming it to be abstract, and Kenny denying that there is anything present at all. The difference between Rorty's and Wilson's positions lies in the sets of cases that they classify to be object directed in the first place. Wilson dismisses as "malfounded"—and does not take them into account in his theory—the cases in which anger or resentment is directed in error. Rorty continues to see them as object directed and adapts her ontology accordingly. A similar nonoverlap prevents a direct comparison between Wilson's and Kenny's views on this question. Most important, while Kenny's units of investigation are subjects having emotions, Wilson's are subject-item pairs. Kenny theorizes about the special nature of emotional states; Wilson, about a specific type of relation that exists between an emotion and its object. The third pairing makes for easier direct comparison because Rorty and Kenny incorporate similar basic conditions within their respective theories.

I make the point that one cannot treat the theories of object directedness as if they were competing theories of one phenomenon. Their differences are partly due to the fact that they are motivated by distinct clusters of cases. It interests me to look more deeply into these differences and to speculate on their origins. The outcome of these speculations reinforces my thesis that there is no natural concept behind the label "object directedness." All we have is a sprawling class of cases that supposedly fits a single category. Because the notion is so weak, those who have attempted to analyze it have had to partially invent the notion to supplement the conceptual threads that were already there. This accounts for the considerable divergence of views. In particular, I believe this suggests the reason behind the significant divergence in the views of Rorty and Solomon, on the one hand, and Wilson and Hume, on the other.

There is clearly an important connection between our emotions and the way we view the world—situations, individuals, and events. On encountering a situation or individual, one perceives it to have certain properties, one believes certain things about it, and one formulates expectations with respect to it. One's emotional response to an individual or situation is determined by the nature of one's attitude towards it. I do not want to enter the already active debate over the nature of the interdependence between emotion and attitude, so I keep my observations modest. Certain beliefs, perceptions, and expectations appear naturally connected to certain types of emotional reactions. One sees someone take one's hard-sought parking space and one is angered. One expects a meeting with an ex-spouse to be difficult and one dreads it. One anticipates the loss of love and intimacy and one becomes jealous.

Attitudes can be ill-founded, beliefs incorrect, and expectations not met. One's vantage point influences the way one perceives a situation or individual. But many point out that it is not the way the world really is that directly determines the nature of one's emotional response, but the way one sees it—one's attitudes, beliefs, and expectations.

I make the assumption that what I have described above is not contentious and with slight variation would be acceptable to any of our theorists. The fact is relevant to object directedness in the role it is given in a theory of object directedness. Rorty and Solomon infuse their objects of emotion with the perspective of the subject having the emotion. We cannot talk about an emotion's object directedness without at the same time providing information about the way the subject perceives the world. The objects of emotion have all those properties that the subject believes them to have. The objects of emotion are not identified with independently existing, extended items because the attributions of properties made by the subject, being inaccurate and affected by the subject's perspective, need not overlap completely with the properties of any extended item. Given the decision to incorporate the connection between emotion and attitude into the conception of emotion, it is easier to see why Rorty notices the explanatory function of the object.

Hume and Wilson choose not to ground the identity of emotions' objects on the way the subject views the world. They view objects predominantly in their role as an emotion's focus. This does not mean that either of the two ignores the importance of the mutual influence of attitude on emotion. They merely fit this fact into a different point of their theories. Wilson takes certain attitudes, beliefs, desires, and so forth, to be partially constitutive of the emotion but sees no need to work this into the identification of its object. Hume, I think, gives appraisal a causal role. For example, thinking about one's friend's generosity causes one to experience love. And we see that he makes much of the conceptual separateness of the two. The object of emotion—if the emotion has an object at all—is an item in the world, with all of its real properties.

The point I have expressed in various ways throughout this chapter is that there is no independent notion of object directedness that we can turn to in adjudicating among these opposing viewpoints. If one sets aside questions of the internal merits of each of the theories, assessing which of the theories projects the *right* notion of object directedness is a matter for stipulation and not argument. Hume and Wilson argue that Rorty and Solomon are wrong because they fail to bring into the picture the items in the world toward which an emotion is directed and inflict upon the conception of the object all this excessive subjective baggage. Rorty and Solomon turn the point around accordingly. I believe that each of these approaches identifies a valid feature of our emotions and with differing degrees of success promotes an account of this feature. But I do not think that any single one of them captures all that has become associated with the label "object directedness." Kenny's catchall specification according to a very general feature of the way an emotion is described leaves us with the feeling that there really is nothing interesting about object directedness. Moreover, one should not overestimate even the formal similarities among the sentences that fit it.[1]   Below, I enumerate and outline some of the phenomena that have until now been swept together under the heading "emotion's object directedness."

3. Dissecting Object Directedness

It is helpful, in forming a new picture, to cease thinking in terms of the duality *emotion-object* and begin to think in terms, rather, of a situation or set of circumstances in which there is an individual having an emotion. I call this an *emotional episode.* I do not limit the notion of a situation or set of circumstances to a small chunk of space and time within which the subject's having the emotion occurs. I would like to extend it to include all those factors that are *relevant* to the emotion. This is the set of factors that bear in important ways on the subject's having the emotion and could even include an event in the subject's distant past, a character trait of the subject, the subject's cognitive state, or another individual. I assume further that it makes sense to include among the components of situations any properties and relations that have bearing on the emotion.

---

[1] See numbered examples and the Appendix.

What other treatments have subsumed under the heading "emotion's object directedness" I express as a fact about distinct aspects of the emotional episode. The emotional episode includes factors from several categories that bear on the emotion in a variety of ways. I shall classify these aspects—also called *factors affecting the emotion*—into categories according to the way they affect or bear on the subject's emotion. Apart from identifying the type of the emotion in an emotional episode—namely, jealousy, hatred, anger, etc.—there are several other aspects of the situation that bear on the subject's emotion in a variety of important ways. In describing the emotion, one frequently includes a description of the features of the emotional episode that are related to the emotion in one or more of these ways. In place of analyzing object directedness I recommend that we examine these categories of factors that constitute emotional episodes and look at the ways in which the factors bear on the emotion.

I attempt to clarify things with the following analogy. Consider the occurrence of an event—say, the crashing of a DC-10 jet. There are a number of factors that one might consider relevant to the crashing of the jet: when and where it crashed, its altitude, how long it had been flying, etc. One might look for explanatory factors, tying the crash to the state of metal joints, inefficient construction, and, going as far back as the planning stages, an oversight by the design engineers. One may refer to the "human factor" when considering if the crash was due to pilot negligence. One might uncover a precipitating cause, a sudden change in air temperature, which exacerbated the structural weaknesses. One could talk of the jet-crash episode, including as part of the episode, or set of circumstances, all these factors. But the factors bear on the jet crash itself in different ways. We would not think of merging the factors together under one concept. Neither would we want to lose the information regarding the relations between the distinct factors to the plane's crashing. The same holds of emotional episodes, although emotional episodes are more complex because they involve psychological as well as physical factors.

In the rest of this section, I discuss a number of the categories of factors represented in emotional episodes. I do not mention some of the more basic factors like spatiotemporal location but emphasize mainly those factors that have provided the material for investigations in emotion's object directedness.

4. Aspects of Emotional Episodes

Relation to a Focus.   An emotional episode may include a special type of relation between the one having the emotion and an item in the world: a person or group of persons, an inanimate item, or an event or a state of affairs—in other words, the concrete items of our common sense world. The item is a component of the situation, that is, the emotional episode, and bears a certain relation to the emotion. I qualify this further by specifying the type of the relation. Emotion and item are related as a result of the item's being the emotion's *focus*. For example, in instances of love, envy, and anger, the emotion is focused on an individual. In instances of regret, shame, and embarrassment, a past action is the focus. In almost all cases of the emotion types mentioned above, the situation involves an item that is the emotion's focus. When we describe emotional episodes, wanting to draw attention to the fact that this relation exists and to the identity of the relatum, we use sentences like the following:

1. Frank loves Susan.
2. Martin is afraid of his neighbor's dog.
3. Phoebe fears the campus rapist.
4. Paul regrets having refused to invest in Apple Computers.
5. Lynne is angry at the man who dented her car.
6. Lynne is angry at Dennis.
7. Julia envies Pamela.
8. Clive is distressed over his business losses.
9. Hannah is angry that she was not invited to the party.
10. Peter fears the headmaster.

In these statements, the focus of the emotion is the designatum of the expression following the emotion verb. I do not offer this as a comment about all emotion sentences of this form. The way one interprets these sentences has as much to do with which emotion verb occurs in the sentence as with more general formal features of the sentence. "David is dreading the meeting with his ex-wife" and "David is dismayed over the meeting with his ex-wife" illustrate this point. The former does not describe a focused emotion because the relevant relatum does not yet exist. This should not be surprising. Kenny's hope that all the necessary semantic information is present in the knowledge that the verb is psychological is naive. Looking at the verbs of cognitive attitudes within this category, the significant differences are evident. Consider sees, seeks, knows, imagines, and hopes. Further, I do not mean to suggest that the sentences 1–10 describe only a relation between the subject and a concrete particular. Some, like sentence 9, seem to provide, in addition, information about the subject's cognitive state.

I have merely suggested one of the factors that is possibly present in an emotional episode. To make the point fully convincing, the suggestion must be supplemented with an analysis of the relation between a subject's emotion and the emotion's focus. In doing this, one notices further subdivisions within the class of possible relata that may be relevant to the analysis one offers. For example, certain types of emotions are more likely than others to involve relations to another individual. This holds typically of loving, hating, resenting, envying, despising, loathing, fearing, and adoring. Past actions are the focus of another set of emotions: remorse, regret, relief, shame, embarrassment, and approval. Certain other emotions are related to events that are not necessarily actions, such as being sad about a disaster or pleased over a victory. I consider Wilson's discussion of the emotion-object relation to be about much the same aspect of an emotional episode as this one, in which case one possible form of the relation of emotion to focus is causal. Hume, too, in a limited setting identifies this aspect of an emotional episode in discussing the objects of emotion. In Part Two, I offer my own analysis of the category of factors I am now calling the focus of emotions. As for the rest of the categories of factors, I manage no more than a brief mention.

Explanatory Factors.   There are concrete items that bear on an emotion but not in virtue of their being its focus. That is, there is another category of factors comprised of items in the real world that enter into emotional episodes. These are explanatory factors. The set of circumstances contains, in addition to an emotion's focus, factors that can be cited in an explanation of the emotion. For example, to explain Lynne's anger, one cites the fact that someone dented her car. In explaining an emotion, one frequently makes reference to a property. One cites the man's aggressive manner in explaining someone's disliking him. There are linguistic expressions that refer to the explanatory factor in an emotional episode. Consider for example:

11. Dorian was resentful because he was overlooked for promotion.

12. The man was embarrassed by his wife's behavior at the party.

One also finds explanatorily relevant information in other types of sentences in which the information is less obviously given. For example, if I say,

"She dislikes the aggressive man" or "She was delighted over her son's victory," I give not merely the emotions' foci. The descriptions used in these sentences refer to features of the man and of the event, respectively, that are explanatorily relevant to the emotions.

In discussing Rorty's views on object directedness, I remark that she merges the concept of an emotion's focus and that of explanatory factor. In these two sections, I have maintained the separation of these two types of factors into distinct conceptual categories.

5. Arguments against Relationality

In the literature on emotion's object directedness, there are four types of arguments given against a simple relational picture of emotion and object. In many ways, the point in contention is very similar to the one concerning the objects of perception. The naive realist takes a position on perception that is comparable to some form of a relational view on the objects of emotion. The arguments from illusion and hallucination brought against the naive realist find strong parallels in the context of the discussion of emotion. I shall discuss the four arguments and then show how this issue bears on the question of further constituents of emotional episodes.

The first argument is a close analogue of the argument from illusion. Imagine the following situation. Lynne returns to a parking lot to find that her new car has a large dent in the left side. She recalls that Dennis, her next-door neighbor, had been parked in the space to the left and that the red paint on the dent matches the red of his Pontiac. Lynne is angry at the man who dented her car, who she thinks is Dennis. In fact, it was after Dennis had vacated the space that a woman named Betsy, driving a red Ford, backed into Lynne's car, causing the dent on its left side.

The example brings out a difficulty for a straightforward relational analysis. Lynne agrees that she is both: she is angry at Dennis and angry at the person who dented her car. However, there is no concrete particular that satisfies both characterizations, that both is Dennis and is the person who dented Lynne's car. Lynne adamantly denies that she is angry at a person named Betsy. These facts point to the conclusion that what Lynne is angry at is not a concrete particular since there is no concrete particular with the attributes being named Dennis and having dented Lynne's car. Since Lynne's anger is no different in this case from what it would have been had Dennis, in fact, backed into her car, it is reasonable to ask for an account of anger and its focus that would simultaneously account for both cases. Because of this, the relational account is clearly inadequate. Whether one *describes* the situation with the statement "Lynne is angry at Dennis," "Lynne is angry at the person who dented her car," or "Lynne is angry at Betsy" is a separate but interesting question.

In a second line of argument against a straightforward relational analysis, many cases of emotion that appear to fit this model are shown not to. More specifically, it may seem to be the case that an emotion is directed to an individual when in fact the key to the emotion's directedness is one of the individual's properties. Or, better still, it is one of the properties that the subject attributes to the individual. In statement 10 above, Peter does not fear the individual who happens to be the headmaster; rather he fears the individual qua headmaster who is stern and strict and believes boys should be punished once in a while. Lynne is not angry at Dennis per se. She is angry at him qua individual who dented her car without accepting responsibility for repairs. One is not proud of the concrete particular, namely, the house on lot number ten; rather, one is proud of the house qua beautiful, expensive item in one's possession. That the emotion appears to be focused on a concrete particular in cases such as these is an epiphenomenon of the genuine relation. The confusion arises when the characteristics grounding an emotion happen to converge on a particular individual—that is, happen to be present in an actually existing individual.

A third reason given for rejecting a simple relational picture is that emotions seem often to be focused on future possibilities, or events that are merely imagined. Among examples already mentioned, fearing a nuclear war, dreading a meeting with one's ex-spouse, and being afraid that one will be attacked by a wild animal in the bush do not differ greatly, in the way we describe them, from ones like loving Susan. But because they are future directed, a relational analysis of their directedness is impossible. The same is true for cases in which an emotion is focused on an imagined event. One might long to go on a date with Anthony Andrews or be horrified over the thought that there might have been another car at the intersection when one failed to stop at the red signal. Amusement, which I classify as emotion, is frequently associated with imagined events. Watching a stately banquet on the television one might be amused at the thought of a waiter spilling food over Nancy Reagan. Much comedy is derived from the situations that someone asks us to imagine.

The fourth line of argument takes off from linguistic considerations. From the examples already given, consider once again the following: "Hannah is angry that she was not invited to the party," "Clive is distressed over the financial losses of his business," "Sheryl is afraid that she will be attacked by a wild animal in the bush," "Sue longs to go on a date with Anthony Andrews." These sentences describe object-directed emotions. If one accepts the claim that their objects are designated by the object-expressions, then they are propositions and not concrete items. This position obviously takes off from a certain approach to the question of interpreting similar belief-statements (and other attitude reports).

These arguments are directed against purely relational accounts of object directedness. Each of them makes the point that a relation between an emotion and item in the world does not account for all the features of object directedness. With this, I am in complete agreement, which is why I offer relationality as *one* of the important factors in an emotional episode. The counterexamples presented above illustrate some of the others.

6. Further Aspects of Emotional Episodes

Relation to a Property. The second argument against relationality cited instances of directed emotions in which the emotion is directed not, it seems, to the individual but to the individual qua possessor of a certain feature. According to my proposal, the two views are *not* in conflict but represent distinct categories of factors that enter the set of circumstances involving an emotion. In a given emotional episode, it is possible that in addition to there being an individual upon whom the emotion is focused there is a certain property or relation with special significance with respect to the emotion.[2] Take Lynne's anger over the dent in her car. I do not want to give up information regarding the identity of the person on whom her anger is focused, or of the *feature* of the person that is relevant to it. Consider the case of a snob who despises someone of a lower social class. The snob does not despise the property *being of a lower social class.* Yet the property features crucially as a factor in the attitude of the snob to the other individual. Again, one wants to give roles of equal importance to the individual and the property. A final example to illustrate the point: Attending a convention, one notices its efficient running and admires the

---

[2] This way of thinking about things avoids the need to posit mysterious types of entities like the man-qua-owner-of-a-mansion-overlooking-the-Pacific-Ocean.

person responsible for organizing it. This is possible even if one does not know who this is. Once again, the admiration one feels is not aimed at the property but at the person. Yet one notes the property as a special feature of the emotional episode. Frequently, when one wants to draw attention to a special property, one uses the appropriate description in referring to the emotion's relata. For example, one reports:

13. I admire the person who organized this convention.
14. She was angry at the man who dented her car.
15. The snob despised his servants.

Conversely, certain types of emotions do not involve both an individual factor and a property. Love exemplifies this in certain situations.

I have made no attempt to analyze the precise nature of the role played by properties in the cases I describe. Is it again a question of focus? That is, is it the fact that the properties play a causal role or is it that they feature in explanations of the emotions? These possibilities would eventually need to be settled by an examination of properties relevant to a subject's having an emotion.

State of the Subject.   There are aspects of an emotional episode that are not traceable directly to factors outside of the subject's state and yet are analytically separable from the emotion itself. The instances of emotion for which this factor is present are themselves quite varied. The cases I cite in illustrating the first, third, and fourth arguments against relationality are ones in which this aspect is present. We are alerted to the fact that this aspect is present in a given emotional episode by certain features of the way the episode is described. I offer the following rough characterization: The object expressions are manifestly descriptions of factors external to the subject but in the context of the emotion are used, in addition, to describe features of the subject's state.

There are three types of these cases corresponding, roughly, to three of the arguments brought against a straightforward relational analysis. One argument consists in pointing to future-looking emotions, and emotions directed to events merely imagined by the subject. I drew the analogy between a second form of argument and the arguments from illusion and hallucination: There is a discrepancy between what the subject thinks and the actual state of his environment. Third, I mentioned the argument that cites propositional emotional attitudes as cases in which a straightforward relational analysis would not work. A few examples should serve to illustrate these types of cases.

First, we have the cases in which the emotion is directed to a future possibility or an event merely imagined: One describes David's dread as "dreading the meeting with his ex-wife," though the meeting with his ex-wife has not taken place. I mentioned cases of amusement, fear, and longing in which the object-expressions described the state of the subject. Relief, regret, remorse, and shame introduce similar factors referring to events or actions that did *not* occur. For example, I can be relieved that the police decided not to press charges of negligence, or I can regret that I did not visit my friend in the hospital. The question of how precisely these object expressions are being used to describe the subject's state is an extremely difficult one. I should stress a point that is always ignored in the literature on emotion's object directedness. It is crucial to give due consideration to the implications for the state of the individual and for the state of the factors in an emotional episode of the *type* of the emotion. For example, dread is always future looking, while fear [3] is on occasion future looking but may also be relational. One can be as relieved about something one has done as about something one has not done. One can long only for something that is not occurrent. Worry is an interesting emotion since one worries over what might be the case. One returns from a meeting and worries that one might have offended someone or one worries that one might have failed an examination.

Second are the cases in which a subject errs in her appraisal of the directedness of her emotion. There is some variation in cases of this type. Consider the application my idea of an emotional episode to the case of Lynne's being angry over her dented car. We have a subject, Lynne, having an emotion, anger. Dennis is one of the relational factors because Lynne's anger is focused on him. But there is another aspect of Lynne's anger. She claims to be angry at the person who dented her car. It is *as if* she were angry at the person who dented her car. One uses "the person who dented her car" to describe Lynne's emotional state even though she is wrong about the identity of the person. Were one to go only by Lynne's subjective state, there would be no way of distinguishing this case from one in which Dennis did in fact dent the car. And this is the aspect of Lynne's state, analytically separable from the emotion, to which I have attempted to draw attention.

---

[3] As in fearing being mugged on one's walk home or fearing that one will be attacked by a wild animal in the bushes.

A variation is exemplified in the case of a man regretting that he ruined his family, when in fact he was not instrumental in bringing about their ill fortune. In this case, we can identify no relational factor corresponding to the expression "that he ruined his family" that enters into the emotional episode. Yet the expression has valid implication regarding the nature of the man's state. It brings out the similarity between the state of the man, in this case, and the state of a man who in fact did ruin his family and regrets it.

Third, there are the propositional cases. I suggested earlier that the statement "Frank loves Susan" expressed the fact that the individual named Susan is a factor in the emotional episode involving Frank's loving—its focus. I suggest further that "Hannah is angry that she was not invited to the party" and "Paul regrets that he refused to invest in Apple Computers" describe a relational factor involved in Hannah's being angry and Paul's regretting—albeit a more complex one. There is more to the second two cases than that. They refer not only to relational factors but describe indirectly the states of their subjects. There are many other types of emotions for which this form of description is appropriate. There is also variation in the forms these more complex descriptions take, as one sees in the following:

16. He was indignant over the poor treatment given to the refugees.
17. She was delighted that her son won the prize.
18. She is sad about having to leave.

In the absence of sufficient background, I must remain vague on what might be included as part of the subject's state. One possibility is that the object-expressions describe the subject's cognitive states. Or they might serve a more general purpose in suggesting the subject's dispositional state. For example, in statement 16 the subject might be expected not only to be thinking certain things but also to be disposed to act in certain ways under certain conditions. These issues are given an insightful treatment by J. Barwise and J. Perry [4] in the context of their discussion of the semantics of belief and perception statements.

Because of the additional factor introduced in statements like "Hannah is angry that she was not invited to the party" they carry information even if Hannah had in fact been invited to the party and through a misunderstanding thinks she had not been. In this case one would add the qualifier "... even though she in fact was invited." We would discount the

---

[4] *Situations and Attitudes*, 1983.

relational information and take account only of what the assertion tells us about Hannah's state.

I stress once more that I have merely mentioned this additional factor possibly present in emotional episodes. A thorough analysis would be needed in order to vindicate this. I predict that a successful analysis will account for the differences that are signalled by the variety of linguistic forms.

7. Conclusion

Of all that has been said about object directedness perhaps the richest source of information is the set of cases of object-directed emotions. If one takes in the full range of phenomena present in this class, it becomes evident why the conception of emotion's directedness has fared so badly in the literature on emotion. It is simply far too varied. The views examined in Chapter 2 reflect this problem. None even approaches a theory of object directedness that covers the entire class of cases. Because the content of the concept far exceeds the limits of a plausible analysis, I propose that we abandon the project and focus attention on the components of object directedness that may be handled in a more systematic way. This decision is not regrettable if one views the class of emotions as a heterogeneous class of mental attitudes and respects their diversity accordingly. In this chapter, I have identified several of the diverse elements that have previously been bundled together under the label "object directedness." I have indicated ways of recognizing these elements on the basis of formal linguistic considerations but have stressed that one must attend closely to the semantic features of individual emotion verbs.

In the remaining parts of this work I develop an analysis of one of these elements, the one I call "relation to a focus." In examining this relational aspect of emotion I am led to reconsider, in a limited setting, our conception of emotion.

PART TWO

Emotion

Chapter 4

Two Theses

There is a view of emotion, partially supported by our preanalytic notions and perpetuated by philosophers and psychologists, that embodies two theses. Below, I introduce the theses and give examples from the literature I have covered of theories that incorporate them, and then I argue that the theses cover only a fraction of our common conception of emotion.

1. The Two Theses

Almost all the theories of emotion that I have encountered embody the two theses to be discussed here. From the perspective of various theories of emotion, the theses might be seen as very general answers to questions such as what in the world corresponds to an individual's having an emotion? or, on particular occasions when we ascribe an emotion to an individual, what precisely are we attributing to the individual? Thesis I asserts that an emotion is a property of an individual involving only the intrinsic features of the individual having the emotion. Thesis II asserts that, in attributing an emotion to a subject, one is attributing to the individual an *occurrent* property. Taken together, the theses assure a common core to all answers to the question of what an emotion ascription amounts to. In attributing an emotion to an individual, one provides information about the individual's occurrent state, making no essential reference to factors outside the individual.

Both theses involve distinctions that have considerable philosophical histories. In elaborating on the theses below, I rely on the intuitive appeal of these distinctions, trusting that my explication will not be affected by troublesome borderline cases. I show, too, that the two theses are independent.

In formulating the first thesis, I presuppose a distinction between predicates that are relational and predicates that designate 'pure' properties. By pure properties, I mean properties that may be identified without reference to another individual. The predicate "is green," applied to the walls of my living room, and the predicate "is in pain," applied to Saul, designate properties that are pure in this sense. "Is the daughter of Karla" is an example of a predicate that is relational. Predicates involving intransitive verbs often constitute cases of nonrelational predicates. These are exemplified in sentences such as "Abby is singing" and "Jock is running," which assert states of their subjects that may be ascertained by observing features intrinsic to them, at the specified spatiotemporal locations.[1]

The idea of an *occurrent* property is roughly this: In attributing an occurrent property to a subject, one is indicating a feature of the subject that may be identified concurrently with the attribution. With this, too, I can pretend to no rigorous formulation. Most important is the contrast I recognize between occurrent and dispositional properties. [2] "Abby is singing," "Saul is in pain," and "The shoes are brown" predicate of their subjects occurrent properties. "This vase is fragile," "My friend is generous," and "The politician is honest" involve dispositional ones. Although the sentences contain present ascriptions of properties to their subjects, they ascribe dispositions to their subjects.

Earlier, I asserted that these characteristics of properties are independent. There are properties that are nonrelational and nonoccurrent; dispositional properties exemplify these. There are properties that are occurrent and nonrelational—for example, "is in pain," "is green," "is singing," "is feeling hungry," "is dizzy." Transitive verbs designate occurrent relations. It is a common practice in linguistic analysis to interpret a transitive verb in terms of a relation. A simple sentence containing a transitive verb describes a relation between the agent, designated by the subject of the sentence, and the object, designated by the grammatical object expression. For example "Sally is touching Rocky" describes a relation between Sally and my cat

---

[1] Relying on intuitive judgments rather than on sophisticated philosophical distinctions, I ignore factors like the primary-secondary distinction whereby even color, for example, is relational.

[2] In other contexts, this distinction is quite explicitly adopted, in particular, in discussions by Hempel and others of dispositional properties in science. Discussions of personality traits have led to conclusions that point to their dispositional nature.

Rocky. There is an event that involves a relation between the two in virtue of Sally's movement. The action of touching is a relation, with Rocky as its object. This contrasts with verbs that are not given relational interpretations. These are classified as intransitive verbs, exemplified in "Sally is sitting" and "Jock is running." An object-expression is not required to complete a sentence containing an intransitive verb. Accordingly, the actions of sitting and running are nonrelational. There is no more to these actions than the nature of the activities of their subjects. In the sentence "Sally is sitting on a chair," the expression "on a chair" does not designate the action's object but an adverbial qualifier. It qualifies Sally's sitting by giving its location.

The expression "Sally's sitting" refers to an occurrent property of Sally's. The sentence "Sally is sitting on a chair" refers to the same occurrent property, except that it is now spatially qualified. The term "sitting" applies to Sally in virtue of Sally's action, which is fully specifiable in terms of intrinsic features of Sally alone. The expression "Sally's touching Rocky" refers to an occurrent relation between Sally and Rocky. Although touching is a relation, it does involve certain occurrent properties—movements that Sally makes. But we limit the term "touching" to the relational notion.

Below and in the chapters that follow, I discuss a class of emotions that are neither pure properties nor occurrent. A further example of a predicate that fits this category is given in "Herbert is generous with his son."

I hold that most theories of emotion portray an individual having an emotion as an episode, or an occurrence at a determinate space time location, involving intrinsic features of the individual. According to Thesis I, an emotion involves the subject alone. That is, the subject's having an emotion may be characterized by reference to intrinsic features of the subject alone. Saying that Stan is angry, for example, I need look no further than Stan for the confirmation of this claim. This does not place emotions in a vacuum. Information pertaining to the emotional experiences of a subject might include facts about the origins of the emotion—its causes—or the rationale proposed by the subject, the object of the emotion, and so forth. But these facts merely *qualify* the emotion, in the way adjectival or adverbial phrases qualify nouns or verbs. Insofar as sentences like "Stan is angry at Ethel" or "Stan is angry because of Ethel" are about Stan's emotions, they are about Stan's current states. The precise function of the expressions "at Ethel" and "because of Ethel" is dictated by the theory one adopts on objects and causes of emotions. Thesis I, that emotions are pure properties, dictates that, like pain and hunger, the intrinsic features of

Stan are all that is involved in his being angry. Thesis II, that emotions are occurrent, dictates that there is currently something that identifies Stan as angry.

Theories of emotion featuring emotions as experiential states of certain types prototypically embody the two theses. These theories portray an individual having an emotion as an individual undergoing certain subjective experiences. As such, the emotion is an occurrent property of the individual: One need look no further than at features intrinsic to the individual to determine the nature of his current experiences. (This is not strictly an epistemological claim.) Hume's idea of a passion as a simple impression of reflexion fits this mold. The theories of Descartes, who sees the passions as "perceptions, or sensations, or excitations of the soul," [3] and of Reid, who sees passions as agitations of the mind, are similarly included in this category.

It is now fashionable to see emotions as experiences that include a variety of mental activities. Wilson envisages an emotion as a complex event, marked by changes in feelings, thoughts, attentional patterns, and impulses to behave.[4] Howard Leventhal, in offering a psychological theory of emotion that portrays emotion as the upshot of a series of cognitive processes, sees the emotion, that which must be accounted for, as a subjective perceptual experience.[5] Magda Arnold, a respected contributor in the field, holds that emotions are felt tendencies toward anything intuitively appraised as good or beneficial or away from anything intuitively appraised as bad or harmful. The attraction or aversion is accompanied by a pattern of physiological changes organized toward approach or withdrawal.[6] Lazarus, a psychologist, puts forward what is seen as a prototype of a component approach to the analysis of emotion. He offers the following definition:

> Emotions are complex organized states consisting in cognitive appraisal, action impulses, and patterned somatic reactions, individu-

---

[3] p. 28. R. Descartes, *The Passions of the Soul*, unpublished translation by Stephen Voss.

[4] J. R. S. Wilson, *Emotion and Object*.

[5] H. Leventhal, "Toward a Comprehensive Theory of Emotion," in *Advances in Experimental Social Psychology*.

[6] M. B. Arnold, *Emotion and Personality*, vol. I, p. 182.

ated and identified on the basis of all three components. The emotion is experienced as a whole, a single experiential phenomenon.[7]

The picture of an emotion as a complex mental event, either an experience or an experience *and* something else, portrays an emotion as occurrent and involving intrinsic features of the subject alone. Therefore, it, too, incorporates the two theses.

James exemplifies another stream of thought, emphasizing the physiological bases of affect. In his view, there is no element of pure consciousness that is identifiable as emotion. Rather, an emotion is the conscious experiencing of bodily changes following the perception of some situation. It is the secondary effect of the eliciting situation, mediated through the bodily changes.[8]   Other "materialist" theorists have preferred to stress purely neurophysiological factors and yet others, feedback from the facial musculature.[9]   Schachter and Singer expounded a theory of emotion that identifies an emotion as a combination of cognitive and physiological changes.[10]   In these views, the emotion continues to be seen as an event—granted, now specifiable in material terms—involving features of the individual having the emotion.

I hold, by contrast, that there is a significant subset of our emotions that satisfy *neither* of the theses—emotions that are nonoccurrent and relational. I am not sure I could motivate the finding that in so large a class of emotions the features of nonoccurrence and relationality converge. The independence of the theses makes it conceivable that there are emotions satisfying one but not the other. If one interprets Wilson's position on emotions directed to individuals to include the claim that instances of emotion specify their objects "up to individual," as discussed in Chapter 1, these emotions are relational and occurrent. Depression could be an ex-

---

[7] See R. S. Lazarus, A. D. Kanner and Susan Folkman, "Emotion: A Cognitive-Phenomenological Analysis," in R. Plutchik and H. Kellerman, *Emotion: Theory, Research and Experience*, vol. 1.

[8] W. James, *Collected Essays and Reviews* and W. James, *The Principles of Psychology*.

[9] See especially C. Izard, in *Human Emotion*.

[10] J. Singer, and S. Schachter, "Cognitive, Social and Physiological Determinants of Emotional States," *Philosophical Review*.

ample of emotion that is nonrelational and nonoccurrent.[11] [12] I limit my discussion to cases of emotion that are both relational and nonoccurrent.

2. Emotional Relations

I argue for my claim that the theses are not valid for all emotions given the common conception of emotion. I do so by describing a class of emotions for which they do not hold. These emotions are neither obscure nor rare yet are almost always neglected in academic studies of emotions. I think they deserve a closer look. I make further use of a subclass of these emotions in the next chapter to illustrate one of the ways emotions effect a relation between a subject and parts of the world—that is, when an item in the world is the focus of an emotion.

I make the case for the existence of nonoccurrent emotional relations in two stages. I first argue that there are sentences legitimately seen to be sentences about emotions, that do not describe *occurrent* properties of their subjects. Second, a subset of the sentences that describe nonoccurrent emotions describe a special kind of relation among their protagonists: emotional relations. In this chapter, I am mainly concerned with the first stage. It is difficult to keep the issues strictly divided since it happens to be the case that many of the nonoccurrent emotions are also ones that I see as relational. In the next chapter, I emphasize the relationality feature in offering an alternative picture of many of the "standard" emotions like love, hatred, and envy. In the final chapter of Part Two, I apply my picture of an emotional relation to the analysis of one of the aspects of an emotional episode, that which I call "relation to a focus."

Under the assumption that emotions are occurrent states of individuals, one expects that simple present-tense sentences like

1. Polly is angry.
2. Selwyn is distressed.

describe a subject actuated by such passions. For the purposes of this argument, I will assume that sentence 1 and 2 indeed assert of their subjects the appropriate emotional characteristics. What one takes these features

---

[11]   Michael Bratman suggested this.

[12]   Bedford's picture of emotions offers another possibility for portraying emotions that satisfy Thesis I but not Thesis II. See E. Bedford, "Emotions," in *Aristotelian Society Proceedings*.

to be will depend on the particular theory of emotion that one adopts. I remain noncommittal on this issue. The assumption I make amounts to taking sentences like 1 and 2 to be descriptions of a state of affairs in which the state of their subjects is identifiable as of the *types* anger and distress, respectively. Interpreted in this way, these sentences are similar to ones like "Cedric is in pain" and "Jock is running."

There are more complex and informative ways of describing emotions than with atomic sentences like 1 and 2. Consider, for example,

1'. Polly is angry because Michael insulted her.
2'. Selwyn is distressed over the baby's crying.
3'. Shortly before the concert he was very nervous.

Yet, insofar as 1'-3' are about their subjects' emotions and insofar as emotions are taken to be occurrences involving only the intrinsic features of their subjects, the sentences say no more about the nature of their subjects' emotional states than do the corresponding atomic counterparts: 1 and 2. The additional clauses in 1'-3' serve to qualify the emotions. "Because Michael insulted her" qualifies by designating an explanatory factor; "shortly before the concert" is a temporal qualifier of his nervousness. They do not add information about the intrinsic features of their subjects' states. According to a two-thesis view, this implies that they give no further information about the nature of these states insofar as they are emotional states. Take the assertion: "Polly is angry because Sally did not return her call." According to a two-thesis view, to determine the nature of Polly's emotional state it is sufficient to examine the intrinsic features of Polly's occurrent state. Moreover, this examination is insufficient to distinguish between Polly's emotion in 1' and her emotion in the assertion above. Qua emotional states, they are identical.

I borrow the idea of an emotion's being qualified by a phrase or clause from the notion of an adverbial qualifier. Recall the example of Jock running. Jock may be running quickly or slowly, he may be running toward the train station or away from his neighbor's fearsome bullmastiff, or he may be running because he is trying to keep fit. The common factor in all these cases is Jock's running. The supplemental expressions are adverbial qualifiers of the action, which is common to all five situations. The sentences "Jock is running fast," "Jock is running away from the dog," and "Jock is running in order to keep fit," refer to the common action, Jock's running. The adverbial phrases assert distinct qualifications of the action. Each asserts something more about Jock's running in the described situations. But according to intrinsic features of Jock's state, the term "running" applies in each case.

Were we to extract from the complex sentences those parts that refer to the emotion or the action component of the situations they describe, we would extract "Polly is angry," "Selwyn is distressed," "He is nervous," and "Jock is running." I call this operation 'detachment'. It is a consequence of the two theses that sentence 1 would be considered the result of detaching the emotion component from sentence 1'. Insofar as the nature of the emotion is determined fully by the intrinsic features of Polly's occurrent state, 1' asserts no more than 1 about Polly's emotion.

I use the notion of detachment fairly loosely here; no doubt it would benefit from more precise specification. I describe as "detachment of the emotion component of a sentence" the operation of extracting from the sentence those parts of it that refer to the emotional status of its subject. On the assumption that an emotion fits the specifications of the two theses, detachment in 1' and 2' yields 1 and 2. This follows from the suggestion that the additional expressions in 1'–3' qualify the emotions, which are already completely identified in the unqualified cases. In detaching the emotion component of a sentence, one extracts that part of the sentence that describes the emotional state of the individual.

The notion of detachment might become clearer if one considers cases in which, as I argue later, it is impossible to detach the emotion component in the simple manner described above:

4. Polly is angry at Michael.
5. Deanne loathes her stepfather.
6. Pamela is jealous of her younger brother.

These sentences are typical of sentences describing so-called object-directed emotions. The challenge is this: Insofar as these are sentences that ascribe emotions to their subjects, is it possible to identify or detach their emotion components in such a way that what is detached designates emotions that satisfy the two theses? This must be answered in the affirmative if one is to continue to support a theory of emotion that incorporates the two theses.

One straightforward attempt to meet the challenge might be to proclaim the detached emotion components to be:

4'. Polly is angry (same as 1).
5'. Deanne is loathful, feels loathing; or something along these lines.
6'. Pamela is jealous.

How one identifies the function of the complementary expressions "at Michael," "her stepfather," and "of her younger brother" will depend on the analysis of object directedness that one adopts. For example, we saw that, in Wilson's view, these expressions designate causal factors involved in the eliciting of the emotional responses. A view like Kenny's in which the object expressions lose their usual referential capacities is consistent with this type of detachment. The expressions function to qualify the emotions. That is, they serve to further specify the episodes in which the subjects are undergoing certain emotions. On the view that sentence 4 makes no reference to any individuals apart from Polly, it is still the case that Polly's ascribed state is one of anger, and so 4′ is an appropriate detachment of the emotion component.

My response to the challenge of making the correct detachment is different. I hold, in contrast, that sentences 4′–6′ do not at all represent the information of 4–6 pertaining to the subjects' emotions. If it is in fact the case that Polly, who is angry at Michael, is also angry, this is a mere coincidence and only an indirect consequence of 4. Polly could be angry at Michael yet, right now, not be angry at all. My positive claim is that 4 and sentences like it have an emotional content quite different from 4′ and other appropriately similar counterparts. I elaborate this claim more fully in the next chapter.

In asserting the relational nature of a certain set of emotions, I intend to draw a parallel between the statements 4–6 and ones that are more straightforward descriptions of relations, like:

7. The Trade Center is south of the Empire State Building.
8. Alison is taller than Betty.

The correct detachment of the emotion component would yield the sentences 4–6 themselves. The argument for the relational character of certain emotions must wait until chapter 7.

I now show that sentences like 4–6, sentences about the emotions of their subjects, do not describe their subjects' occurrent states. In particular, they do not yield 4′–6′ as their emotion components. To make this point, I tell a story about one Paul M., the subject of a fictional psychological study. The conditions of this story are designed so as to bring into focus a feature of a significant class of emotions, which is reflected in the way we talk about them. Furthermore, I argue that this is not merely a "manner of speaking" but corresponds to an aspect of our conception of emotion that is not covered by sentences like 1, 2, and 4′–6′. That is, there are emotions that do not satisfy the two theses.

A team of social scientists investigating emotion makes a study of the emotional life of the "average" male individual, Paul M. They gather a wide range of data from behavioral observations, interviews, paper and pencil tests, and so forth. On the day August 26th, 1982, they write a report. I use "*t*" to refer to this period. The passage following is an excerpt, *R*, from the fictional report:

> Paul M. loves Suzie W., is angry at Jane F., is delighted about his recent promotion. He is proud of his new car, despises his
> *R* landlord, is ashamed of his behavior at the office Christmas party, and is worried that within the next five years the world will be destroyed in a nuclear war.

Setting aside serious doubts one might have over the scientific import of these seemingly anecdotal findings, it is sufficient that *R* is seen to be neither incoherent nor inconsistent—logically or synthetically. Now the challenge: What is the detachable emotional component of *R*? A proponent of Theses I and II, following the reply to the earlier challenge, might suggest that a similar straightforward detachment is possible:

> Paul M. is feeling love, is angry, is delighted, is proud, is
> *R′* feeling ashamed, and is worried. [It is not clear how to adapt appropriately the fact that he despises his landlord.]

Suggesting that *R′* is detachable from *R* in constituting its emotional component is to suggest that, insofar as *R* is about Paul M.'s emotions and insofar as emotions are occurrent and nonrelational, *R′* adequately captures its emotion content. It follows that if R is true of Paul M.'s emotions, so is *R′*. Now, however, the apparently trite set of observations in *R* seems transformed into a quite remarkable fact about our average Paul M. He is, concurrent with the writing of the report, experiencing no less than seven distinct emotions—that is, under the assumptions of the two theses.

Several questions arise in light of the nature of this transformation. Does it indicate that we performed an erroneous detachment in *R′*, because, whereas *R* is perfectly coherent, *R′* is not? Or is *R′* symptomatic of a mistake underlying any view of emotion that incorporates the two theses?

One might argue that *R′* is not the appropriate detachment of R because *R′* is incoherent, whereas *R* is not. But this argument is effective only if we agree a priori that it is possible to experience only one emotion at a time. Then asserting *R′* is as bad as asserting that there is a surface that is red and green all over at the same time.

If one rejects the hypothesis that an emotion experienced at a given time must be unique, then the line of argument above will not work.[13] The simultaneity is surely not of crucial importance. (I happen to think that, even if we agree that the emotion experienced need not be unique, it is still highly implausible that a person is experiencing *seven* simultaneously.) In this case, we might see the move from R to R' as equivalent to that from

A Jake is standing in the living room, leaning against the bookcase, sipping a dry martini.

to

A' Jake is standing, leaning, and drinking.

There is no inconsistency in this. However, if one tacks onto the end of A "Jake and Minnie are waltzing around the dance floor," the coherence of the passage is disturbed. We know that, as a matter of fact, it cannot be true simultaneously of one person that he is standing, leaning, drinking, and waltzing. This fact underlies the incoherence of the appended A and of the equivalently appended A'. The idea is that, were we to judge R' incoherent, we would not judge it so a priori, based solely on the fact that it attributes simultaneously to Paul more than one emotion. If so, it would be equally true of R that *it* is incoherent. Yet we recognized at the outset that R was perfectly reasonable.

Above, I have examined one attempt to challenge the validity of the move from R to R'. This involves pointing out that, whereas R is coherent, R' is not. I argue that the challenge is unsuccessful since, if we recognize the possibility of ambivalence, or more generally the possibility of experiencing more than one type of emotion at any given time, the claim that R' is incoherent may not be defended as an a priori consequence of our conception of emotion. Arguing that the move from R to R' is prevented not in principle but by virtue of the material impossibility of R'—given our factual knowledge of the world—is equally unsuccessful. To make the argument from 'matters of fact', one notices the equivalence of the claims expressed in R' with claims about a certain individual's simultaneously standing and waltzing. The strangeness in these claims is not a feature of the claim that the individual stands and leans simultaneously.

This argument does not work. Whereas in appending the waltzing clause one affects the soundness of A as well as the soundness of A', R

---

[13] Greenspan, in an article in A. Rorty, *Explaining Emotion*, argues that ambivalence is a distinguishing feature of emotion; that is, we are able to experience, simultaneously, contrary emotions.

seems a perfectly reasonable and innocuous observation. If the apparent queerness of R' were due to the fact that the emotions mentioned in it are incompatible, then R should also be troublesome. Yet, as I said initially, R exhibits none of this incoherence or inconsistency. The move from R to R' still stands and as such poses a threat to a two-thesis view. Since the move from R to R' seems to be what is most straightforwardly implied by the two-thesis view, it remains its burden to block it.

Detachment of R' is not something we would expect as a consequence of any successful theory. Consider whether the following facts would be taken to have any bearing on the truth of the reports R and R' respectively: During period t, Paul M. went to work, watched a football game on television, and slept soundly for six hours. I believe that there is a perfectly good reading of R with respect to which these facts are completely irrelevant. The same may not be said of R', given a supporting theory of emotion that complies with the two theses. If the truth of R' is threatened by these additional facts, which in no way bear on R, this argues against the possibility that R' is implied by R.

It is worth noting as an aside that, although my argument deals explicitly with the inference from R to R', I think that it would apply equally well to other attempts to interpret R as a passage about occurrent properties of Paul M. Whatever the set of sentences proposed as the emotion content of R, if it comprises sentences ascribing occurrent properties to Paul, it is vulnerable to precisely the form of argument I have given against R'. This new R'', whatever it may be, would fly in the face of the assertion that Paul M. is asleep.[14]

In any case, if one could talk of the intentions of fictitious social scientists, it is clear that they do not intend their report to be valid only for the period t. This is consistent with the point I argue above, where I show that R is not a report about occurrent properties of Paul M. Yet I continue to maintain that R is a passage about Paul M.'s emotions. The conclusion

---

[14] This is very much in the spirit of the point Ryle makes in *The Concept of Mind* about dispositional and occurrent mental attitudes. However, it is not sufficient to let the matter rest there because (a) Ryle is committed to a behaviorist interpretation of mental concepts and (b) the dispositional, or nonoccurrent, nature of emotion is rarely acknowledged. I share his inclination to interpret many types of mental attributions as reported inductions on complex patterns of phenomena. I think a more convincing case can be made for this without the behaviorist restrictions.

toward which I am working, but cannot quite draw, is that the emotions in R are not occurrent. In addition, I hold a relational view of these emotions, but here I do not argue for this. Those wishing to continue to hold the view that emotions of the types mentioned in R are occurrent have yet another tack. Before I consider its merits, I should indicate in more realistic terms what sort of cases the Paul M. example is intended to represent.

The Paul M. story, I admit, is farfetched. Nevertheless, it represents a mundane and frequently encountered characterization of our own emotions and those of others. Without giving a thought to what activity a friend might currently be engaged in, we would be confident to report certain facts about his emotions, for example, that he misses his family, is disappointed he did not get the apartment, or is afraid of his neighbor's dog. Or take, for example, the gossip that is passed by those who are interested about the advice columnists and twin sisters Ann Landers and Abigail Van Buren. It has been 'reported' that they have been angry at each other and not on speaking terms for ten years. One surely does not imagine that this describes the columnists' occurrent states for the duration of the ten years. One would probably think that during that time they experienced certain feelings, acted in certain ways, said certain things, held certain beliefs, and so forth. Such would be the grounds for believing that they had been angry at each other over the ten years.

There have been other philosophers who have recognized an alternative conception of emotion to one that is completely captured by the Theses I and II. Lawrence A. Blum, for example, in his book *Friendship, Altruism, and Morality* draws attention to the episodic and nonepisodic uses of emotion terms. He writes:

> Someone can have compassion, concern, or sympathy, on specific occasions, fairly well delimited in time. But to 'be concerned about' and to 'have sympathy for' do not refer to distinct emotion episodes.[15]

He holds that we can *be* concerned about something at some time but not then *feel* concern. He also adds what I consider to be an interesting caveat, that the expressions "having compassion for X" and "feeling compassion for X" can both be used either episodically or nonepisodically. In other words, we should not see the distinction he is indicating as one merely about labels. Yet he says little beyond this about the origins of the distinction. In

---

[15] *ibid.*, p. 13.

a footnote he stipulates that nonepisodic occurrences of emotion terms are not simply ways of referring to dispositions to the parallel feeling states.[16]

This mention of a dispositional interpretation anticipates a framework within which a substantial portion of my discussion below takes place. Blum says tantalizingly little about the possibility of interpreting nonepisodic occurrences as dispositions. Wilson is another who points out that emotion terms are used to refer to facts about the emotions of individuals that are not facts about their current states. He also mentions dispositions but, in my opinion, is hardly more informative than Blum in showing how they are brought to bear in explaining the nonepisodic uses of emotion expressions. I shall give a brief account of Wilson's comments on "nonoccurrent" emotions and then show where this leaves us with respect to the initial problem of interpreting R and, in particular, identifying the nature of its emotion component.

Wilson. Wilson notes that there are mental reports that appear to refer to dispositions rather than to occurrent states of an individual. Belief reports, he claims, are predominantly of this nature. Pain reports are of the opposite kind. He places reports of feeling emotion in the second category: "To feel an emotion is to be in a phenomenal state of mind."[17]

Wilson acknowledges that there are cases that appear to be attributions of emotion having no implications for the current mental state of the individual—that is, we are calling dispositions "emotions." About these dispositions Wilson writes:

> When we refer to such a disposition as an emotion, rather than as an attitude, we perhaps imply that the person must be disposed to feel in certain ways, and not just to behave and think in certain ways.[18]

Wilson judges that these are not what we in general intend when we talk about emotions, saying, "We have in mind such actual states or feelings rather than dispositions."[19] He chooses to ignore the latter in proposing an analysis of the emotion-object relation.

If Wilson decided to concentrate on emotions that are conscious states because of his supposition regarding their overwhelming frequency, he made

---

[16] *ibid.*, p. 208, fn 3.

[17] J. R. S. Wilson, *Emotion and Object*, p. 70.

[18] *ibid.*, p. 76.

[19] *ibid.*, p. 76.

a poor choice. I am inclined to say that he underestimated the importance and prevalence of talk of dispositional states that are emotions. Perhaps this reflects the focus of most of the academic work on emotion rather than what is true about emotion. In any case, I do not have the empirical evidence to support my hunch, so I shall say no more about the question of the relative frequencies of dispositional and occurrent uses of emotion terms.

More relevant to the central question is that Wilson does acknowledge that certain emotion reports do not describe the ongoing experiential states of their subjects. Furthermore, he identifies emotions so reported as dispositional mental properties, much like beliefs. Apart from the passage I quoted above, Wilson offers no further specification as to what he sees to be at the bottom of the distinction between occurrent and nonoccurrent emotions. Below, I shall frame some questions that direct us once more to the puzzle about the interpretation of the Paul M. story and similar cases.

I begin by taking Wilson and Blum together. From what I have reported, do we conclude that they come to conflicting conclusions on the nature of these nonepisodic emotion reports? Wilson says they report dispositions; Blum denies this. Does all this talk about dispositions have anything to do with the Paul M. story and other expressions that do not appear to report on the occurrent states of their subjects? I answer these questions below.

Dispositional Properties Versus Dispositions to Have a Property.
Recall the problem. We have seen that R' does not capture the emotional facts in the report on Paul M., R. I question whether this is to be taken as evidence against the idea that emotion satisfies the two theses. The puzzle for one who wants to defend the 'traditional' view is to explain the way of speaking about emotion that R exemplifies. Is it a challenge to the two-thesis model, or is it a mere 'manner of speaking' that, if properly interpreted, can be defused? An answer seems available in taking further the idea of emotions as dispositions, hinted at in the writings of Blum and Wilson.

I draw attention to features of the way we talk about action to illustrate a point about the description of dispositions. Given an agent, Harriet, it is possible to assert at a location, l, that Harriet is singing at this location, with "Harriet is singing." This ascribes an occurrent property to the subject. The sentence

9. Harriet sings in the shower.

does not. The simple present tense gives us the capacity to report on a current disposition of the subject. In denying that sentence 9 describes a current action of Harriet's I am not denying that singing is an occurrent activity. It is just that language affords us the capability of talking about an agent's habits, abilities, and dispositions to perform these actions. In the case of 9, we are being informed of Harriet's habit to sing, conditioned on a location, the shower. Whether or not Harriet happens to be sleeping at l has no bearing on the truth of 9. I use the phrase "disposition to have a certain property" to refer, in general, to what it is that sentences like 9 assert about their subjects.

This bears on the puzzle in the following way: One who chooses to defend the two theses says of the sentences in R that they do not report on the current emotions of Paul M. but on his *disposition* to experience the emotions mentioned. Then one can admit that R' does not represent a detachment of the emotional component of R without giving up the two theses. Report R' is an incorrect way of detaching the emotional component because it fails to incorporate the dispositional nature of R. In the model of disposition to act, R is seen as a report on the disposition of Paul M. to be angry, to feel love, to feel shame, to feel pride, and so forth. And none of this is affected by knowing that at the time of the report's being written Paul M. was engaged in a number of completely unrelated activities. In the same way that one need not give up the idea that singing is a current activity, one is able to preserve the universal applicability of Theses I and II to emotions.

I have said nothing about how the phrases "at Jane F.," "Suzie W.," "about his behavior at the office Christmas party," and "of his new car" function. Presumably, they would have to function in some way to qualify the occurrence of the parallel emotional states, qualifying the contexts of occurrence of the emotions along the same lines that "in the shower" qualifies the occurrence of Harriet's singing. I do not feel inclined to offer a more thorough account of their function because I think that this way of reading R is misguided. I do not think, for example, that saying that Abby was angry with Ann for ten years reports only the fact that during that period she was disposed to being angry. Further, it is not obvious how one would work in "with Ann" as a qualification on the occurrence of anger.

My rejection of *this* interpretation should not be seen as an all-out rejection of dispositional readings of sentences that are about emotions. For example, a sentence like "He worries about his daughter" or "He enjoys her company" seems to me to be about the subject's disposition to worry or to enjoy her company. Neither does the rejection of the interpretation suggested above reflect a blanket rejection of any dispositional interpretation. I think that there is another way of claiming that R says something about Paul M.'s dispositions that is more promising. For this, I do not use action as a model but dispositional predicates.

Earlier, I talked about dispositional properties. Consider the following:

10. The vase is fragile.
11. The senator is not easily corrupted.
12. My friend is generous.

In sentence 10, for example, a current attribution is being made to the vase. The property referred to by the predicate happens to be a dispositional one. Being fragile disposes the vase to be affected in certain ways, like breaking or cracking, by certain modes of treatment, like dropping or rough handling. It is not the case that 10 is dispositional because it describes a situation in which a vase is disposed to being fragile. This example brings out what I take to be a valid distinction between a sentence that attributes to a subject a *disposition to have a property* and one that attributes to a subject a *dispositional property*.

The difference between the two as applied to emotion is this: In the first case one is attributing to the individual a disposition to have an emotion, but in the second case one attributes to him an emotion, where the emotion *is* a disposition. In both cases, one is able to explain why there is no danger of incoherence in R, but, in the first case only, one is also able to do so without disturbing a commitment to the truth of the two theses. If one adopts the proposal that the sentences in R attribute to Paul M. dispositional properties and that these *are* emotions, then one effectively contradicts Thesis II.

In fact, I have not quite accurately described my view. I support a variant of the second case. The variation enters in the following way: I propose that sentences like those in R describe relations. The relation between the subject and referent of the object phrase displays characteristics that incline us to call it dispositional. This picture no longer fits Thesis I, either.

Right now, it is difficult to see how I could argue conclusively against the first possibility offered of a dispositional reading of R. I hope that it appears as implausible to others as it does to me. I depend on more realistic cases such as the one involving Ann Landers and Abigail van Buren to convince others of the validity of my preference. I do not find it disconcerting that

I have no knockdown argument against it because, first, I think there *are* occasions in which it is an appropriate mode of interpretation and, second, in order for someone to support it as a serious alternative, they would have to stipulate the role of the "qualifying" expressions and generally fill in details. Meanwhile, I shall develop my suggestion in the hopes of offering a plausible case for it in this way. That is, I intend the advantages of my theory of emotional relations to weigh in favor of my approach, over the dispositional reading discussed above. In particular, the analysis of emotional relatedness helps clarify the troublesome issue of the so-called object directedness of emotion.

Before moving to the explication of my positive proposals, I make a few concluding remarks directed to the questions I posed earlier about the views of Wilson and Blum. Despite appearances, their views on nonepisodic emotions are not obviously in conflict. Blum denies the equivalence of a nonepisodic assertion that someone is concerned about X and the assertion that the person is disposed to be concerned about X, episodically. This is in accord with my view that reports of nonepisodic emotions do not report dispositions to have those emotions. Wilson, too, does not explicitly commit himself to this implausible dispositional hypothesis. At least superficially, the dispositional interpretation he affirms is more in line with the type that I support. In the next chapter, I spell this out more fully.

The status of the two theses in light of the preceding discussion is this: Insofar as a two-thesis view yields the types of implications illustrated in the example of Paul M.—the move from R to R'—the view must be rejected. To guard the integrity of the two theses, one might give a dispositional reading to the problematic sentences, holding language responsible for the initial confusions. I reject this move. It seems far closer to our ordinary ways of thinking about the emotions in question that we interpret the sentences to be about emotions that are themselves dispositional or nonoccurrent, and relational. The sentences do report the dispositions of their subjects to have the emotion designated by the verb phrase, but they report an emotion that *is* itself a disposition. In the two chapters that follow, I say more about the nature of these dispositions. *This* picture is patently at odds with a two-thesis view. The argument given in this chapter is directed against Thesis II, the thesis that emotions are universally occurrent. I provide evidence for the relational nature of certain emotions in the final chapter. In the next chapter, I focus on a subclass of these nonoccurrent emotions, including love, hatred, and envy, showing them to be relational, as well.

Chapter 5

Emotional Relations
and the Active Emotions

In *The Philosophical Investigations*,[1] Wittgenstein offers us a contrast: "'For a second he felt violent pain'—Why does it sound so queer to say, 'For a second he felt violent grief'? Only because it seldom happens?" The discussion in the preceding chapter should serve to answer Wittgenstein's question, to explain the queerness of the idea of a second's violent grief in the face of the real possibility of a second's violent pain.

The idea that an emotion is an occurrent property of the individual who is having the emotion dominates traditional theories of emotion, both in philosophy and in psychology. This covers a wide range of theories including those that take emotion to be a type of subjective experience and those that posit emotion as a type of bodily upheaval. The view of emotion as a type of occurrent property promotes the comparison of emotion and sensation, pain in particular.

In the preceding chapter, I argued that, for a broad spectrum of emotions, this view is wholly unsatisfactory. On carefully considering the nature of the emotion attributions made in statements like the following, I recommend that the picture of an emotion as an occurrent property must be revised:

1. Paul loves Suzie.
2. Paul is angry at his mother.
3. Paul is delighted with his recent promotion.
4. Paul is ashamed of his behavior at the office Christmas party.
5. Paul despises his landlord.

---

[1] (Book II, i).

Statements 1–5 might be true, holding simultaneously of the same individual, Paul. It would not matter what Paul is doing over the period that these statements are said to hold. Were he peacefully sleeping at the time that these attributions were made, this would have no bearing on their truth. The same could not be said of assertions such as:

6. Paul is in pain.
7. Paul is hungry.
8. Paul is playing football.

In Chapter 4, I argued that, though 1–5 are statements about Paul's current emotions, they do not describe his current state. My proposed alternative is to interpret "Paul loves Suzie" to be about a relation between Paul and Suzie, one that is dispositional in nature. In other words, this amounts to the claim that the emotions in question are nonepisodic and relational. An emotion is a relation between the designated subject and object.

My hypothesis, namely, that there are nonoccurrent, relational emotions, challenges the belief that the two theses are true of all emotions. It does so not only with a few scattered cases, but also by putting forward emotions that are prototypical of their category: love, hatred, anger, loathing, envy, and shame. In other words, there is a significant class of emotions that may not be distinguished as particular types of occurrent features of the individuals having these emotions. However, my hypothesis is also not universally true of the set of emotions. For example, being enraged, exhilarated, amused, or furious certainly seem to be occurrences.

If emotions, like love, hatred, and envy, are *not* occurrent properties, what *are* they? This is the question to which I now turn. Our common ways of talking about emotions make the traditionally held picture implausible. I propose an alternative picture of these emotions. In taking them to be emotional relations, this picture offers a way of making sense of common parlance. To simplify matters, I restrict my enquiry to a group of emotions that is only a subset of the ones to which my earlier arguments applied.

1. The Active Emotions

The set of emotions that I label "active emotions" is derived from a formal characteristic of the way we talk about them, exemplified in the following sentences:

9. Daniel loves his father.

10. Tilly loathes her boss.
11. Jake adores Minnie.
12. The poet abhors violence.

The principle for deciding whether a given emotion is active is a linguistic one. It should be possible to designate the emotion by a transitive verb in the active voice. Further, the subject of the verb should refer to the individual that we think of as the one 'having' the emotion. Emotions like anger, embarrassment, and fright satisfy the first condition, but in the active voice the subjects of these emotion verbs is not the one who is having the emotion. Consider, for example, "Michael angers Polly." Emotions like jealousy, joy, fury, and indignation fall outside the category in failing to meet the first condition. Loathing, adoring, despising, and abhorring are all instances of active emotions. Envy and fear are counted as active in spite of having nonactive forms in addition to active ones, as "is envious" and "is afraid."

I choose to focus on the active emotions not because I believe that what I say about emotional relations applies to these ones only. Neither is it essential to my position that the stipulations regarding certain active emotions should apply across the board, to all. They provide a suitable domain within which to formulate my position in that the way we speak about them makes a relational interpretation seem quite obviously the right one. Nonactive emotions do not have this advantage. An opponent might take "Polly is angry at Michael" and declare that "Polly is angry" makes reference to the appropriate property. The parallel for "Daniel loves his father" is not at all obvious. The relational nature of love is clearly indicated. Nevertheless, the motivation for my restriction to active emotion is mainly expediency.

To further simplify, I adopt a few nonessential conventions. First, I use the phrase "subject of the emotion" to designate the individual whose emotion it is, the individual referred to by the term in the subject position of sentences like 9–12, about active emotions. Second, I assume throughout that the subjects of emotions are human individuals, designated by proper names, definite and indefinite descriptions, pronouns, and demonstratives—the expressions one would use to answer a *Who* or *Whom* question.

Here are a few additional sentences about active emotions:

13. Julia envies Pamela.
14. Paul regrets having refused to invest in Apple Computers.

15. The captain fears a reprisal.
16. Jeff hates the man who killed his father.
17. Mary admires Agnes.

I illustrate the details of my account with an example of envy. I am confident that it is generalizable to most active emotions—and at least for those emotions designated in the numbered statements.

2. Emotions as General Phenomena

I hold that the statements in my examples do not each describe a particular occurrence, because the emotion verbs they contain function on a level of greater generality than this interpretation suggests. That is, the emotion concepts are general, and so the statements assert general facts. The idea I develop has the flavor of Wittgenstein's suggestion in the following passage:

> "Grief" describes a pattern which recurs, with different variations in the weave of our life. If a man's bodily expressions of sorrow and of joy alternated, say with the ticking of a clock, here we should not have the characteristic formation of the pattern of sorrow or of the pattern of joy.[2]

The idea that my position shares with Wittgenstein's comment is the idea that some emotions are patterns of episodes. In the case of the active emotions, this will usually be a pattern of interactions. A particular emotion is characterized by a complex pattern. It covers a sequence of episodes, all of which 'fit' this pattern. In other words, when we 'cash out' our emotional relation in terms of events, or episodes, we find that it may involve a sequence of heterogeneous activities.[3] Rather than being a means of summing over these episodes, the emotion concept is a way of covering them at a more abstract level. In settling on a description involving a term of emotion, one identifies the 'rule' behind the disparate episodes. A particular event is not so much a *part* of an emotion as something that *fits* it, as, for example, a single note fits a melody. This view is not to be

---

[2] *Philosophical Investigations* Book II, i.

[3] It is possible to cash out the emotion in terms of other sorts of phenomena, such as beliefs, desires, and values. However, in some views—my own included—these phenomena are also nonepisodic, which would involve complex issues that I want to avoid.

identified with those of Wilson and Marks.[4] Although both acknowledge the complexity of emotions, they maintain that the phenomenon is a particular, though complex, event. Thalberg's "component" approach is more similar in that it characterizes an emotion as having a variety of activities as components. His theory comes as a solution to a debate that would take us too far afield to discuss here.

In my view, an emotion is a complex, structured interaction between an individual who is the subject of the emotion and another individual or part of the world. A fact about an emotion is general in that it spans several episodes. For example, knowing what love is, or understanding the conception of love, involves knowing the nature of a pattern over time; it involves knowing which sorts of episodes fit the pattern and which do not. Worrying about a person's well-being typically fits the pattern, actively thwarting his goals rarely does, and greeting him as you pass in the hallway is somehow irrelevant to the relation. Below, I expand on the idea of a general fact and then show in some detail how this characterization applies to facts involving emotions.

General Facts.   I claim that the facts captured in assertions like "Jake adores Minnie" and "Julia envies Pamela" are of a general nature. This might be surprising since on the face of it these are claims about particular individuals, little resembling assertions that are uncontentiously of a general nature. I place in this category claims like "All ravens are black" and "Facial expression is an important feature in the perception of emotion in others." The claim about ravens is general not only in that it covers a plurality of ravens, including the ones in your backyard and the ones alive today, but all ravens past, present, and future.

The claim about facial expressions is more complex. It incorporates several claims that are themselves general in nature, since it ranges over people (and it might include other animals as well), over assorted circumstances, and over a variety of types of facial expressions and their correlative emotions. It could be seen as a conjunction of several general claims: A furrowed brow signals anger, an upturned mouth signals joy, a gaping mouth signals surprise or terror, and so forth.

Facts may incorporate reference to a particular and yet be general, as in "The present South African government mercilessly punishes those it recognizes as threats to the system." (I take it that the present South

---

[4]   J. R. S. Wilson, *Emotion and Object*, Cambridge University Press, 1972; J. Marks, "A Theory of Emotion," *Philosophical Studies, 42* (1982) 227–242.

African government is a particular.) This generalizes over occasions and threatening individuals or parties. The assertion "Peter eats eggplant" involving the single individual Peter is nevertheless general in that it covers a sequence of events of a certain type. It is an instance of a dispositional claim and comes close to the way in which I propose we interpret claims about active emotions.

Having set forth a few examples of other assertions of a general nature, I now turn to the question of the respect in which ascriptions of emotions, like the ones given earlier in the numbered examples, are themselves ascriptions of a general nature. If they share a feature with a claim like "All ravens are black," it is certainly not obvious how they do so. I divide the explication of my claim into two parts, motivated by two broad questions. The first question directs attention to the type of general fact that a fact about emotion is. I hope to defend my claim regarding the general nature of a claim like "Julia envies Pamela" by offering a sufficiently comprehensive characterization of it. The question of the type of the general claim settled, the second question focuses on the nature of the corresponding particulars. Peter's eating eggplant at midnight in Paris is a particular event corresponding to the general, dispositional claim, while a black raven is an instance of the universal claim about ravens. What parallels these in the case of emotions? Can we think of an instance of envy, an envying? Absurd as it might at first seem, my view supports something like this. Seen on a grander scale, my view constitutes an alternative framework for the study of a certain significant class of emotions.

Before attending to the first question, I outline a scenario that I use to exemplify theoretical claims.

A Case of Envy.   Julia and Pamela are now colleagues in a law firm, having graduated from the same class at law school. Julia's activities in and perceptions of the firm are marked by a particular relationship with Pamela. Among the events that characterize this relationship are the following:

- Julia notices that Pamela is assigned interesting and prestigious cases, while she is assigned routine divorce cases.
- Julia frequently thinks about the job inequity, certain that Pamela's salary is higher than hers and that Pamela's prospects for advancement within the firm are better than hers.
- Julia thinks that she is at least as talented at the job as Pamela.
- She fantasizes about a situation in which she has all of Pamela's privileges and good fortune.

- She gives poor evaluations of Pamela's performance and complains of her own situation to family and friends.
- Julia becomes easily agitated and upset when thinking about or discussing her and Pamela's relative standing in the firm.
- When she sees, thinks about, or hears of some particular success that Pamela has met with, she experiences unpleasant feelings.
- When opportunities present themselves for Julia to thwart Pamela's progress in some way, she takes them.
- Julia is acutely attuned to information about her and Pamela's relative standing in the firm. Where this is present in a situation, she will notice it. That is, this type of information is salient to her.

In other words, many of the events involving Julia in the context of the law firm, and many also involving Pamela, fit the descriptions given above.

A scenario exhibiting the characteristics above is accurately described by the statement "Julia envies Pamela." The statement labels the entire pattern of episodes for as long as the interactions between Julia and Pamela continue to fit it. It is reasonable to ask how one determines that a pattern of interactions represents a particular emotion type, that is, how one knows to apply "envy," say, and not another emotion label, to a given pattern of interactions. One major factor in associating the type of the emotion with a particular pattern is the conceptual content of the emotion. Being able to judge a priori that Julia's grumbling over the fact that Pamela's office has a better view than hers fits an envy pattern, and that Julia's pressing the elevator button at Pamela's request does not, reflects an underlying common grasp of the notion of envy. The type of the emotion is not the only factor that determines the pieces of the pattern in any instance of it. In the latter part of this chapter and in Chapter 7, I elaborate on this issue. Now, I turn to the question of how an analysis of the concept of envy yields insight into the structured interaction one finds in particular instances of this emotion.

"Invidious comparison" is at the core of envy.[5] The envier focuses on a particular feature of the envied individual and compares himself to the other unfavorably along this dimension. The inequity strikes the envier as undesirable, discomforting, perhaps even unfair or unwarranted. A wish that the inequity did not exist goes along with these judgments. One may assert that envy involves a *desire* for the envied feature or envied

---

[5] This phrase is taken from Jerome Neu's insightful article "Jealousy" in A. Rorty (ed.), *Explaining Emotions*. In fact, many of my remarks here have been influenced by a section on envy in this article.

possession, but this point is a contentious one. Neu, for example, seems to think not, offering two points in support of his position. First, the envied feature might not be transferable, such as is the case for sparkling blue eyes, beauty, a charismatic personality. It would be irrational to desire to have these nontransferable features. Second, there is a separate species of envy, malicious envy, which involves the desire to equalize by depriving the one envied of the feature or possession.

Against the first point, we might say that the envier does not want the other's blue eyes, charismatic personality, and beauty but merely *wishes* he had features *like* them. Or perhaps it is what one earns as a result of having features like these that the envier desires. This he may rationally desire. Malicious envy, involving the desire to deprive the envied individual of the envied possession, seems more a consequence of unrequited envy turned to resentment. Or perhaps we might distinguish malicious envy from ordinary envy precisely on the basis of the desire. It is not clear which of the two positions is more plausible. I leave the issue with two points. First, there *is* admiring envy which does involve the wish to be raised to the level of the envied individual along the dimension of the envied property. Second, if desire for the envied possession is too strong a condition, a possible weakening of the condition is to require that the envier place a value of some kind on the envied feature.

Envy defines three central roles, that of the envier, the envied, and a feature or possession of the one envied, over which he is envied. [6] In other words, envy is a three-place relation, involving the subject of the emotion and two relational factors: another individual and a property or an item that is in the possession of the envied individual. The three places are needed in order to preserve the freedom of the three central roles to vary independently of one another. Julia does not envy everyone in the firm whose status she perceives as higher than hers. She envies *Pamela* alone.

This sketchy analysis of envy should give the rationale behind one's seeing that certain types of episodes belong to the pattern of an instance of envy and certain types do not. It explains why one sees episodes in which Julia compares herself unfavorably on the envied dimension with extreme displeasure as pieces of the pattern of envy and not, say, love. We may view

---

[6] Actually, there might be several envied features, but I restrict consideration to those cases which involve only one. Even if there is only one, the way we individuate it might involve several particulars identified under a more general description.

similarly her attempts to close the gap between them by either elevating herself or thwarting Pamela. Understanding the concept of envy enables one to recognize these episodes not as unrelated but as items that fit into an abstract mold. But knowing only that Julia envies Pamela does not provide one with sufficient information from which one can reliably infer the details of their interactions. Each instance of envy differs as a result of features of the setting and the individuals involved.

Patterns and Constraints: Two Philosophical Paradigms. I turn now to the first of the two questions: What kind of general fact is a fact about an emotion? I detect two distinct ways in which a fact about an emotion is general. First, it is a fact about an existing pattern of episodes. The emotion concept covers the pieces of the pattern abstractly. Second, the emotional relation involves constraints on situations that include the subject. One may describe these in terms of a set of conditionals. In this, emotional relations bear a resemblance to complex laws. I explain these in turn.

Begin by considering a train of events at the level of particular episodes, that is, from 'the bottom up'. At this level, one construes certain of the episodes in such a way that they are identified with other spatiotemporally distinct episodes. Notably, distinct events may be events of a single type. For example, one notices a change in the leaves on many trees, from green to gold, red, and brown. The change is a recurrence of changes that had taken place at about the same time the previous year, and years prior to that. Distinct, temporally distant events, are drawn together under a single conceptual classification. Another way that an event is deprived of its conceptual uniqueness is if it is seen to be a part of, or a *piece* in, a pattern or 'design'. The leaves changing color is a part of the pattern of changing seasons. Thus seen, it is tied conceptually to the shortening of days, dropping of temperatures, and so forth. Our notion of "autumn" covers this pattern.[7]

Consider another example. A man, Francis Dobbs, enters a store and buys musk essence. He rubs this onto the handle of a Norwegian knife that he had purchased shortly before that. He smears the blood of a dead

---

[7] We would not want to say that "autumn" refers to certain days in the calendar year, first, because autumn does not coincide in the northern and southern hemispheres and second, because autumn may be longer or shorter in different years and at different latitudes.

rat on the blade of the knife...[8] These distinct events fit the pattern of Dobbs's preparing to murder Pratt, the man who is blackmailing him. It takes several episodes to allow us to recognize the pattern, to begin to see that there is an overriding conception that ties the events together. Once the pattern is detected, the episodes are seen to be pieces of it.

The notion of "preparing to X" is used in a variety of domains to cover a pattern of episodes. Take a less gruesome example of someone involved in preparing for a dinner party. David, our protagonist, is currently engaged in chopping onions, having already decided on a menu, shopped, tidied his apartment, invited the guests, and defrosted the chicken. He must still roast the chicken and bake the tart. Instead of giving a phase-by-phase description—"now he is doing the shopping, now he is wiping the table, now..."—one says, "David is preparing for a dinner party." This description covers at a more general or abstract level a collection of episodes that, less abstractly conceived, are distinct. Though all are instances of "preparing for a dinner party," only one is an instance of "chopping onions," one an instance of "roasting chicken," and so forth. Notice that these episodes are distinct not in the way two snowflakes or two identically molded stainless steel spoons are distinct. It does not require careful scrutiny or an examination at the molecular level to notice this. Rather, there is a very ordinary level of conception at which the pieces of a preparing-for-a-dinner-party pattern are distinct. Once we recognize that the episodes are pieces of a particular pattern, we may identify them under one, more abstract, notion. This allows us to point at David chopping onions and say, truthfully, that he is preparing for his dinner party.

I stress a point made earlier, that in using descriptions such as "preparing for a dinner party" one moves up a level of abstraction. It is not simply that one uses it as an abbreviated means of referring to a conjunction of several descriptions. One actually adopts a new level of description, as in moving from species to genus descriptions.

It is a feature of moving to a more abstract level of conception that one loses some of the details of the constituents of the pattern. The information that David is preparing for a dinner party might be all that I want to know about David's activities. Still, there is no denying that I no longer know whether he is cooking quiche or chicken. In fact, it is often possible to

---

[8] See especially p. 162 in "A Case of Premeditation" by Austin Freeman in *The Great British Detective*, Ron Goulart (ed.), New American Library, New York, 1982.

reconstruct the pieces of the pattern from the general information and other facts such as knowing that David is a vegetarian or that he is a gourmet cook and impeccably tidy. The same would be true of Dobbs's preparing to murder Pratt.

The idea that an emotion concept is general, covering a pattern, applies to the case of Julia envying Pamela in the following way: In asserting that Julia envies Pamela over job standing, one describes more abstractly a pattern of interactions that characterizes their relationship. One recognizes that a certain sequence of episodes—Julia becoming furious on hearing their boss praising Pamela, Julia resentfully acknowledging the inferiority of her working conditions, and so on—are pieces of a larger pattern. The disparate events cohere under one classification. The fact that *this* instance of an envy relation is characterized by episodes of the types described in the previous section is determined partly by the nature of the envy relation, partly by the nature of the setting, and partly by features of the protagonists. As with other moves in the direction of greater abstraction, one may not be able to reconstruct all information about the particulars from the general information.

Information is lost in the case of emotion when one moves from individual conceptions of particular events to a more abstract conception of the entire pattern, because the *type* of the emotion does not fully determine the nature of the episodes involved in a given instance of emotion. The framework common to various cases of an emotion is frequently rather sparse. In a particular case of emotion, the features of the individuals involved and the emotion's setting greatly influence the nature of the episodes one finds in the pattern. For example, two cases of envy could vary because of the individuals' cultural backgrounds, personality and character traits, past experiences, and abilities. The locale and the opportunities for interaction among the relata are further determining factors. I speculate that there is considerable variation among emotions in the extent of the similarity between instances of the same emotion. Love has many widely different forms; resentment offers less room for variation. The smaller the contribution of the general notion, the more we lose in using it to characterize the pattern.

In suggesting that emotion concepts in claims about emotional relations serve to identify a *pattern* among a particular set of events, I apply the paradigm of the relation of a piece to a pattern to explicate the relation of a single episode to an emotion. I have not yet told the whole story, for another paradigm seems to model the connection between emotion and these key events equally well. It is an amplification of the relation of a lawlike generalization to its instantiations. I call the function suggested in this second paradigm the "constraining function" of an emotion concept. According to the first paradigm, an emotion concept is an abstraction over a complex pattern of episodes. According to the second paradigm, when one asserts the existence of an emotional relation it is as if one is asserting the truth of several conditionals.

I included several cases of laws or lawlike statements among my examples of general statements. "All ravens are black" is one of these. It is frequently suggested that the best way to interpret universal, lawlike statements is in terms of counterfactual conditionals. In other words, the universal claim is translated as a conditional claim. "All ravens are black" is translated: "If something is a raven—has the property of being a raven—then it will have the property of being black." I use the term "constraint" to capture the conditional nature of these general claims. My reason for applying this term is that, insofar as the counterfactual conditional is true,[9] it imposes constraints on the nature of the world. It does so in that it ties together certain features, or precludes the cooccurrence of others. One sees this in the example of the black ravens. The law constrains the world in that it binds together the properties of being a raven and being black. I intend the term "constraint" to be functional irrespective of metaphysical biases—that is, whether one accepts the idea of necessary connections out in the world or prefers Humean austerity in this regard.[10] Drawing on the parallel between statements about emotions and lawlike statements, I adopt the corresponding notion of an instance. A black raven is a *positive instance of*, or *instantiates*, the lawlike generalization. I do not want my use of the term "instance" to be confused with its use in distinguishing an instance from a *type*. "Instance" in the sense used in my discussion originates with the idea of a positive instance of a law.

A claim like "Julia envies Pamela" imposes constraints on the world in that it conditions certain types of states of affairs upon others. It is more complex than many of the examples of lawlike statements that one encounters in the philosophical literature in that it involves a plurality of

---

[9] I make the assumption that some sense can be made of this idea.

[10] The term "constraint" has a technically precise meaning in *Situations and Attitudes* by J. Barwise and J. Perry. With further specification, my use of this term should coincide with theirs. The vague introduction to the notion given here should suffice for purposes of explicating the second conception of the abstract nature of emotion terms.

distinct conditional statements. The instances of an emotional relation are not prima facie instances. In the case of Julia's envy, the episodes in the pattern instantiate the following set of conditionals:

- In all situations in which information is present, relevant to the relative standings in the firm of Julia and Pamela, Julia notices it.
- In all situations in which Julia is faced with Pamela's success in her job, she becomes unpleasantly aroused.
- In all situations in which Julia has a reasonable chance of thwarting Pamela's progress, she takes it.
- And so forth.

If at a meeting Julia votes against a motion that Pamela proposes or when asked by her superior passes an unwarranted negative judgment on Pamela's performance on a case or feels depressed when she overhears their boss praising Pamela, the envy relation is thereby instantiated. These situations are instances of the envy relation because their features cohere in just the way that the conditions stipulate. Julia had the opportunity to frustrate Pamela's advancement and she took it; similarly with the other cases. Carrying over from the law analogy, these events are seen as positive instances of the law.

The analogy with lawlike generalizations may be carried somewhat further, in particular in the way laws are cited in explanations. One frequently sees an emotion cited in explanation of an observed phenomenon like an action. One might say, "She refused the invitation to his party because she despised him." Instead of accounting for the viability of this explanation in terms of a causal link, one sees it, according to my theory, as a case of explanation by subsumption under a generalization. Similarly, the paradigm supports the predictive power of recognizing the presence of emotional relations. These ideas would require a more careful development than I am able to give them here.

I compare statements about emotions to dispositional claims insofar as they convey the constraints on the interactions and activities of the individuals referred to. "Peter eats eggplant" reports on Peter's disposition, which is to eat eggplant under the *right* conditions—whatever these may be. Statements about emotional relations make complex dispositional claims because they, too, carry information that, in situations of such-and-such type, the protagonists will engage in the corresponding activities. "Julia envies Pamela" is a complex dispositional claim because it reports on Julia's disposition to act in certain ways, experience certain feelings, and notice certain things, if certain conditions are met.

Up to this point I have tried to establish the claim that our emotion concepts are general concepts,[11] the particulars being events. Attributions of emotion may be related to sequences of events in two ways. An attribution of emotion is an abstraction over the sequence in which the named protagonists feature. This collection of events is seen to form a pattern to which an emotion term applies. The type of the emotion does not fully determine the nature of the pattern of which the events are 'pieces'. Features of the individuals, and the setting, contribute significantly to this. The second way events are related to emotions is in being constrained by them. Emotion attributions entail a conjunction of counterfactual conditionals. This imposes constraints on actual occurrences in requiring the correlation of certain sets of features with certain others. In envy, someone else praising the envied individual over possession of the envied feature arouses displeasure in the subject. According to the case of envy that I outlined, Julia's thwarting Pamela's advancement when the opportunity has arisen instantiates the emotion, while Julia's going out of her way to be helpful to Pamela is a counterinstance to the conditionals I suggested.

Until now, I have switched back and forth between talking of emotion dispositionally (especially in Chap. 4) and in terms of its patternlike quality. It is time to bring the two paradigms together into a coherent picture of the nature of emotion and to state the connection between the two functions of emotion attributions. Are emotions patterns, are they dispositions, or are they both? I hold to the third alternative. But it is not obvious how the two paradigms can be combined in the characterization of a single phenomenon. I explicate this below, anticipating possible problems my proposal raises.

One puzzle concerns the divergent existential implications of a dispositional interpretation and one that takes an emotion to be a pattern. If an emotion attribution refers to a pattern of episodes, it implies the existence of at least some of its pieces. If one takes the assertion "Julia envies Pamela" to be describing a pattern of events one, implies that at least some parts of it have occurred. A dispositional reading of the statement has no such implication. It tells us only that, *if* certain events take place, then so will certain others, or *if* certain features are present in a certain situation, it is bound to be the case that certain others are present. It involves no

---

[11] At least, those that fall in the class of active emotions.

existential commitment. The two interpretations appear to conflict with one another.

There is no real conflict, for, although the dispositional interpretation has no existential implication built into it, it does not preclude the existence of the appropriate events. Its only function is to stipulate restrictions on any episodes that might occur. Although the combination of paradigms is not precluded at so superficial a level, the need to explicate the connection—if any—between the two functions of emotion attributions remains. Till now I have suggested two paradigms for the interpretation of claims about emotional relations but have given no hint as to their simultaneous workings in a particular instance of emotion. Statements like "Julia envies Pamela" and "Daniel loves his father" describe a pattern of events using abstract terms and suggest constraints on possible events involving the individuals they designate. How does one reconcile these two descriptive functions? Or, to put this question a bit differently: I maintain that a statement about an emotion both describes an existing pattern and suggests constraints. To ensure the defeasibility of this supposition, a minimal requirement on consistency must be met. In other words, we should have reason to believe that, if a particular emotion report describes a certain pattern, the pieces of the pattern are not be counterinstances to the conditionals that this same emotion report implies; and vice versa. Before I attend to this issue and finally show the interaction of the two paradigms in the conception of emotion, I review some of the main points covered in the chapter.

3. The Picture Thus Far

In the limited setting of the active emotions, I hypothesize that facts about emotions, and emotional bearings to persons and parts of the world, are general facts. This raises several issues. One is the issue of the nature of these 'general' emotional facts. Another is a concern about the nature of the particulars. An obvious third factor to consider in this vein of questioning is the relation between the general fact about the emotion and its corresponding particulars.

The particulars in an emotional relation are events featuring the subject of the emotion and other persons or parts of the world. A speculation, which I develop in the next chapter, is that the events of an emotional relation fall into three major categories: thinking, acting, and feeling. Events are relevant to emotions in two ways, one of which is in being pieces of a pattern, where the pattern includes a variety of types of events. The emotion concept picks out the pattern at a more abstract level than the conceptions under which its pieces are distinctly identified. For example, the distinct episodes of Julia grumbling over Pamela's promotion and Julia feeling outraged on hearing her boss praising her rival are identified in both being pieces of the pattern described by "Julia envies Pamela." Emotion concepts provide an efficient way of classifying a complex, and usually important, relationship between individuals and among individuals and other parts of the world.

A second way in which events are relevant to emotions is in instantiating them. I showed the relation between events and emotions to resemble the relation between a lawlike generalization, or disposition, to its positive instances.[12] The emotion constrains the interactions of the relevant factors. This is simply another way of saying that, in positing that a subject stands in an emotional relation to various items in the world, one posits that the interactions between the subject and the item satisfy a set of conditions. One uses the emotion concept open-endedly to capture a set of counterfactual conditionals. Julia's voting down Pamela's motion at a meeting instantiates the conditional that if given the opportunity to thwart Pamela she will. This conditional is a component of the Julia-Pamela-job-standing envy relation because it accords with the common conceptual demands of envy. Certain information about the protagonists and the setting further influences one's expectations regarding the nature of the conditionals.

I have insisted that the emotion labels apply, strictly speaking, to the abstract conception, in covering the patterns and implying the set of constraints. I concede that in practice this is not always the case. Love may "well up" in one's heart, one may feel pangs of envy or regret, and one may be "clutched by fear." These are not counterexamples to my picture but instances of a derivative use of emotion terms. It is often convenient to apply a more abstract conception to a phenomenon, where possible. For example, one describes David's chopping the onions with "He is preparing dinner." This way one conveys the information that the episode is a piece of a particular pattern. But, of course, there is more to preparing for a dinner party than chopping onions. Similarly, one applies the more abstract emo-

---

[12] Thalberg also uses the term "instance of" to capture a picture that moderately resembles mine in "Constituents and Causes of Emotion and Action," *The Philosophical Quarterly*, vol. 23, no. 90, January 1973.

tion label to an event that is actually a piece in the pattern of the emotion. One describes Julia glaring with hostility at Pamela with "She is feeling envious." Guilt provides a very clear example of a term whose application to a feeling is derivative. We can well imagine that a certain type of feeling is identified as guilt because it is what one feels when one *is* guilty. Being guilty has, of course, little to do with one's emotional state. Yet, now, guilt is numbered among our very basic emotions. Zajonc, whose work features prominently in the psychological literature on emotion, refers to "emotions such as surprise, anger, guilt or shame"[13] and therefore clearly subscribes to this classification of guilt. I think this explains the appeal of a range of claims appearing in the philosophical literature about the nature of emotion. They analyze emotion in terms of other types of mental phenomena. For example, emotion is seen to be a system of judgments, a pattern of salience, and a disposition to certain behavior or certain types of feelings. I offer an explanation of the apparent plausibility of these theories: They work because of the possibility of applying the label of a general notion to the particulars covered by it.

4. Patterns and Constraints: The Connection

I asserted earlier that statements like "Julia envies Pamela" and "Daniel loves his father" contain information of both a dispositional and a descriptive nature. The statements are descriptive in that the emotion labels in cluded in them cover particular patterns of episodes; they are dispositional because they predict certain responses in the appropriate circumstances. These two uses of the statements are not mutually exclusive as are the possible uses of an ambiguous term whose meaning is fixed one way or another depending on its linguistic context. In most cases, in asserting emotional relations one conveys both the dispositional and descriptive information. To maintain this theoretical position, I show that it is coherent, and in doing so I explicate the merging of the two paradigms.

The puzzle over the distinct existential implications of the two paradigms was shown to be surmountable. However, a further consistency requirement must be met. I must ensure that the events that fit the prescribed patterns are not counterinstances to the constraints that the

---

[13] R. Zajonc, "Feeling and Thinking: Preferences Need No Inferences," in *American Psychologist*, p. 152.

emotion imposes and that the dispositions involved in any emotion do not involve events that do not fit its pattern. Instead of meeting the challenge head on, I engage in speculation on how emotion concepts might have acquired their two uses. This should quell some of the worry over consistency as well as anticipate a further question as to whether the mutual consistency of the two interpretations is a stroke of luck, or is a result of a systematic connection between them. I support the latter.

I give epistemic priority to the descriptive use of ascriptions of emotions. General notions serve the useful purpose of unifying and organizing a mass of information. Conception on a more general plane increases our capacity to communicate and store information about a greater number of particulars more efficiently than if we did not have them. Even if, for example, one is not willing to clutter one's mind with the facts that David is chopping onions, has tidied his living room, has been to the grocery store, and so forth, one might nevertheless find it valuable to know that he is preparing for a dinner party. Similarly, knowing that Daniel loves his father summarizes in a useful way the types of interactions that characterize Daniel's relationship with his father.

Certain of our general concepts acquire additional powers. In noting the pattern that characterizes love relations over many pairs of individuals and over the ages, as the astute commonsense scientists that we are, we notice regularities and posit connections. We see not only that people in love frequently experience certain feelings but that they experience them *in response to* certain types of stimuli. We see a person's actions as sometimes having had something to do with a particular feature of the environment—for example, Julia's voting one way having something to so with the fact that it was Pamela who proposed the motion, or Martin's taking the longer route to the store because the fearsome bullmastiff runs loose along the shorter one. The constraints become superimposed on the pattern reflecting lawlike connections in and between the episodes that are its pieces. This explains how claims about emotions come to have both uses. The consistency requirement is met because the conditions introduce no new events to the patterns; they are superimposed on those already present.

An emotion is a pattern of events. There are a number of factors that determine, in a given instance of emotion, the nature of the pattern. The type of the emotion determines the types of the events comprising the pattern. This is seen in the case of envy. The frequency and concentration of certain types of events are another definitive factor. The discussion of constraints points to a further factor: The events in an emotion pattern satisfy certain conditions. Certain types of events follow certain other types of events, and certain properties inevitably cooccur. This constitutes the dispositional character of an emotion. Finally, the events that comprise an emotion pattern involve, systematically, certain individuals and parts of the world. I elaborate on this feature in Chapter 7, where I offer a derivation of the emotion-focus relation.

5. Conclusion

In Chapter 2, I argued that nonepisodic emotions form a significant subclass of emotions. In a more general setting, I echo Wittgenstein's disanalogy between pain and grief. In this chapter, I have offered an alternative to the episodic reading of claims involving these emotions. If in order to establish the presence of an emotion one indeed needs to look for a pattern over time, Wittgenstein's intuition in finding strange the alternation of sorrow and joy is vindicated.

The vindication of Wittgenstein has not been my major, or even a significant, motivation in giving the account of emotions as general notions. I have attempted to close the gap between the analysis of emotion and the conception of emotion that is reflected in the way we commonly report on emotions. This has brought me into conflict with the conception of emotion that has for so long been the subject matter of academic pursuit.

I undertook the examination of the active emotions as a means of better understanding one of the aspects of emotion's object directedness. Statements 1–14 are not only about typical active emotions but about typical instances of object-directed emotions. My analysis of the active emotions yields, further, an analysis of their object directedness. More accurately, it offers a way of analyzing the relation of an emotion to its focus. I explicate this in the final chapter. In the next chapter, I speculate on the types of episodes one typically classifies under emotion concepts.

Chapter 6

Pieces of the Pattern

In Chapter 5, I gave a general description of dispositional emotional relations, calling them abstractions over patterns of events, that imply constraints on and between these events. In this chapter, I follow through on my proposals in two directions. First, I discuss the implications of my analysis of the active emotions for a comprehensive theory of emotion. I examine ways in which my alternative conception of emotions like love and envy affects the goals of a theory of emotion. Second, I fill in the picture by making substantive suggestions regarding the nature of the events that typically instantiate emotional relations.

Before taking up these two points, I introduce several notions in order to facilitate further discussion. Envy, anger, disgust, love, and fear are *types* of emotion. Given a type of emotion E, an instance of this emotion type, e, occurs in a *context*. The context consists of the subject of e, any individuals related by e to the subject, and the setting of e. The *setting of e* is the location of e defined in terms of spatial or temporal variables or with markers that are more descriptive. The setting is the changing environment within which the relata are embedded. I have chosen this way of partitioning the emotional episode[1] for the special case of active emotions with individual relata. The setting together with the context comprises what in Chapter 3 I called the set of circumstances of the instance of emotion. Consider how this partition applies in the case of Julia's envy. The context of envy includes Julia, the subject Pamela, their relative job status, and a setting. The setting could be defined in terms of a date and place or with more descriptive markers, such as "the office of the Smith & Smith law firm."

---

[1] See Chapter 3 for a definition of this term.

In Chapter 5, I remarked that from the type of emotion alone one cannot deduce the nature of the events nor the set of constraints satisfied by the events that constitute a particular instance of it. As one's knowledge of other factors increases, one's ability to predict the episodes and constraints becomes more and more reliable. I make the dependencies more specific using the notions introduced above. Think of the context and emotion type as two parameters in determining an emotional relation. As we fill in more information about the parameters, our knowledge at the episodic level increases. In other words, the theory of emotional relations offers no rigid connection between the type of the emotion and the array of episodes and constraints that the emotion concept covers. Consequently, particular instances of envy, love, dread, and hatred vary significantly from one another. The theory predicts that the variation will, however, be systematic subject to the nature of the type of the emotion, features of the relata, and features of the setting.

The advantage of my theory of the active emotions is that it offers a realistic view of these emotions, one that makes sense of many of the things we say about emotions. I believe that it is of potential benefit to empirical theories of emotion in that it maps emotion to the theories' real counterparts in the world and not to the simplistic artifacts of observation techniques. The disadvantage of the theory is that it complicates the domain of study. A comprehensive theory of emotion that covers active emotions has its goals redefined to accord with the new structure of emotion. It can no longer isolate *the occurrence*, an emotional response, and list the characteristics of the occurrence. The new study of emotion begins with a conceptual investigation and then ascertains the systematic connections among the type of emotion, the variation in context and setting, and the episodic outcome of a particular instance of the emotion. A theory either is aimed at the general notion of emotion or focuses on a particular emotion.

If one were to make a focused study of envy, for example, one would begin with the concept and try to answer questions like the following: Does one envy the other individual or the other's feature or possession? Does envy involve a desire? Does it presuppose an accurate assessment of the relative standings of the envier and the one envied? Can one derive the moral value of envy from a conceptual investigation? With the concept firmly in one's grasp, one moves to consider the possible forms of instances of envy. One might ask which characteristics of the envier interact with envy to determine the nature of the episodes and constraints. A controlled individual may not carry out antagonistic actions directed toward the one she envies; a devious individual may take indirect moves to achieve the desired possession. The setting, too, determines the face of envy: the family in cases of sibling rivalry, the workplace in cases of envy between colleagues, social circles in case of envy between rival suitors or best friends. To study the effects of a single parameter, one fixes the others and sees how the nature of the events and constraints is influenced by variation in the first.

For the time being, the comprehensive theory must wait on more basic questions of theoretical stage-setting. I turn to consider the question of what emotional relations are made of. Emotion concepts of love, envy, fear, and so forth classify sequences of events, enabling us to identify patterns among them. The concepts, in addition, imply conditions on and between the events. I hypothesize further that the range of events comprising emotional relations is not completely open. One does not look at a rainstorm as a possible piece in an emotion pattern, nor a situation in which the subject is being woken by her alarm clock. The events that are classified and constrained by emotional relations fall into three general categories: thinking, acting, and feeling. More specifically, the sequence of events conceived of as an emotion involve the subject of the emotion in thinking, acting, and feeling. I break no new ground in positing an association between emotion and these three human capacities. The novelty lies in the way I characterize the association, the idea that emotion concepts classify *patterns* of events involving thinking, acting, and feeling. I discuss these categories below. Events involving thought, action, and feeling that fit into a pattern of an emotion also satisfy the appropriate set of conditions. I illustrate these as they affect a number of types of emotions. I conclude this chapter with a discussion of salience, or selective attention. In the literature on emotion, this phenomenon is frequently bound up with the conception of emotion. My picture offers a way to explicate the connection between the two.

1. Thinking

The role of thinking in emotion and the role of emotion in thinking have long been the subject of conceptual and empirical examination. Magda Arnold, R. S. Peters, George Mandler and R. S. Lazarus are among the many who champion the definitive importance of thinking to emotion. My picture, although greatly influenced by the insights of their views, is distinguished from them in not incorporating the two theses discussed in Chapter 4. My view coincides with theirs in that it gives thinking a constitutive role in emotion.

I use the term "thinking" generically to cover a broad range of mental activities. It covers remembering, calculating, deciding, noticing, interpreting, daydreaming, imagining, apprehending, and more. I prefer to use the term "thinking" rather than the term "cognition," which has entered the vocabulary of many modern investigators. I prefer "thinking" for its associations with a rich philosophical and commonsense tradition. Despite the suggestion of greater precision and its ties with a scientific approach, the term "cognition" is the source of much confusion. For example, debates over the role of cognition in emotion often turn on the misunderstanding of, or disagreement over, what cognition is.[2] Thus it lacks the common appeal without the advantages of an *actual* increase in precision. I classify appraisal, judging, and evaluation as ways of thinking. This might be objectionable to someone who judges appraisal itself to be an affective response. Although I recognize the difficulties involved in drawing lines between the dimensions of like/dislike, good-for-me/bad-for-me, and good/bad, I assume that at least some form of evaluation falls within the category of thought.

My analysis of emotional relations involves only two levels of conception: one in which events are conceived of individually and another of greater abstraction, in which I place emotion concepts. The pieces of an emotion pattern are events. Thinking enters into the analysis of emotion in that events involving the subject in certain forms of thinking are frequently pieces of the pattern and are constrained by the conditions. I therefore limit my interest in thinking to real-time phenomena. I focus on events in which a subject is currently engaged in thinking. This cuts out classifications of mental states that are of a dispositional nature, in spite of the fact that they fit the more general class of human thought. This includes belief, knowledge, understanding, and some forms of desiring and judging.[3]

---

[2] I refer especially to the debate between Zajonc and Lazarus.

[3] I think my analysis in terms of events is not inconsistent with the possibility of a different kind of analysis in terms of other abstract and dispositional notions. Ultimately, however, were one to spell out this new type of analysis in terms of single events, one would expect it to reduce to mine.

The content of a subject's thinking determines its part in an emotion pattern. By the content of thinking I mean the individuals or parts of the world about which the subject is thinking and *what* the subject is thinking about these individuals or parts of the world. Holding fixed the contextual variables, one may associate certain ways of thinking with certain types of emotion. An instance of a hatred relation could involve the subject's thinking about the individual she hates, thinking about the despicable characteristics or deeds of the hated individual, and figuring out ways of avenging herself. The case of Daniel's loving his father suggests a quite different pattern of events: Daniel thinking about his father, wondering whether his father is well, deciding to send his father a card on his birthday, remembering the pleasant days of his childhood, thinking about his father's generosity and fair-mindedness, and concerning himself with his father's well-being.

It is not the content of thinking alone that determines the existence and type of an emotional relation. My approach introduces an additional dimension to the identification of an emotion: the pattern. There is no single episode that constitutes an active emotion. One instance of hateful thinking does not constitute a hate relation. The concentration and frequency of certain ways of thinking about another individual determine the presence of an emotional relation as much as the content of the thoughts.

The subject's thinking is constrained in accordance with certain conditions. In the case of Cindy's loathing Gary, one notices correlations between what Cindy thinks and features of the situations in which she is placed. Given a situation in which Gary's presence is imminent, Cindy thinks of ways she can avoid it. On any occasion on which Cindy is reminded of Gary, she recalls his aggressive manner, condescending tone of voice, bad taste in clothing, and messy eating habits. Paul's regretting that he refused to invest in Apple Computers shows in his thinking whenever mention is made of personal computers: He recalls the events leading to his decision and fantasizes about how his life might have been different had he chosen otherwise. In general, the dispositional information covered by an emotion concept concerns the way the thoughts of the subject are conditioned on certain factors in a situation. This includes features of both the environment external to the subject and the subject's state of mind. Certain trains of thoughts characterize the state of mind of the individual who is the subject of an emotional relation.

2. Action

The pattern of an emotional relation includes episodes with the subject as an agent in much the same way as it involves the subject engaged in thinking. Certain types of actions are characteristic of certain emotional relations. A subject's actions are also constrained in certain ways by both environmental factors and the subject's state of mind. In conformity with the picture outlined above, the actions and constraints on actions for a particular emotion are determined by the type of the emotion and features of the context. One is not surprised to see a lover act to further the goals of a loved one or to protect the loved one from possible danger. But not all lovers send lavish gifts or write poetry in praise of the ones they love. A few envious subjects thwart the attempts of the one envied to greater accomplishment along the envied dimension. Some merely become ill-tempered. Most individuals avoid contact with a person they loathe.

The dispositional element of an emotional relation is reflected in the case of action in the obvious way. One acts to avert possible danger for a loved one, even if this is to one's own disadvantage. One fulfills the request of a person one fears or admires. A remark made by a person one resents elicits a sneer. One objects to the suggestions of an individual one envies. Once again, these constraints are not universally true of every case of resentment, love, fear, admiration, and envy. For example, in some cases of envy the setting prevents the envier from intervening in the life of the one envied. I offer a warning that one should not impose a causal interpretation on the relation between the emotion and the action. It is not the case that the emotion is a causal factor in bringing about the action. The actions and the conditions that the actions comply with are part of what determines the presence and type of the emotional relation.

The active emotions are so named for the formal resemblance they bear, in the way we talk about them, to actions. A transitive action, or emotion, verb in a simple sentence refers to the action or emotion, respectively. The agent is designated by the subject of the sentence, while that which is acted upon is designated by the object expression. Similarly, the subject of an emotion is designated by a subject expression and its focus by the object expression. In a particular instance of emotion, many of the actions it involves match the emotion in that the agent is the subject of the emotion and the object of the action is the focus of the emotion—as in "Frank loves Susan" and "Frank embraces Susan." This match is not coincidental but forms the very basis of emotional relatedness. This observation is the key to my analysis of 'relatedness to a focus', which I discuss further in the next chapter.

3. Feeling

The pattern of events fitting an emotion label usually includes events in which the subject experiences feeling. I give more detailed attention to this category because, of thinking, acting and feeling, feeling is possibly most important in our conception of emotion. This supposition is reflected in the views of the many who either identify emotion with feeling or at least see them to be closely tied phenomena. As in the cases of action and thinking, certain adaptations of these views are necessary in order to place the role of feeling in the new picture of an emotional relation. Before I explicate this, I discuss several general questions connected with the notion of feeling and the role it plays in the conception of emotion. For purposes of this discussion, I set aside the picture of emotion as a complex relation.

In drawing the connection between feeling and emotion, one possibility is that emotion *is* a type of feeling, a subspecies of feeling, alongside pain, warmth, dizziness, hunger, nausea, and 'butterflies in the stomach'. Love, hatred, anger, and delight would be subtypes of emotional feeling. I refer to this suggestion as the naive feeling hypothesis. Below, I examine the substantial content of the hypothesis, consider the evidence for and against it, and see to what extent various historical figures who have written about emotion have supported it.

If the naive feeling hypothesis is right, then whatever we know about feeling must be true of emotion as well. Without attempting to provide a definition for the concept of feeling, I will assume that there is basic agreement in answers to the question "What is feeling?" Even if we are unable to characterize it fully, we are able to recognize a feeling when we see it or, rather, when we have it. Knowing what a feeling is has nothing to do with the physiological correlates. Perhaps in the distant future neuroscientists will be responsible for changes in our conceptual thinking, but until then I use "feeling" to pick out an experiential phenomenon. Having some idea of the distinguishing features of feeling gives substance to the naive feeling hypothesis. It helps to identify the differences between a feeling hypothesis and a conflicting one and what it implies about the nature of emotion. In the absence of a full-blown analysis of feeling, conceptual or phenomenological, the next best thing is a list of 'facts' about feeling.

I offer below some of the characteristics that are frequently associated with feeling. It will be clear that many are not features of feeling exclusively:

1. Feelings are elements of conscious experience, identifiable by introspection.

2. Feelings are not under direct voluntary control. I include the qualifier "direct" to allow for the possibility that feelings are under indirect voluntary control. Descartes discusses this in connection with the control one has over pupil size. One can control pupil size indirectly by focusing on near or distant objects or by moving from a brightly lit to a dimly lit environment. Perhaps one can alter one's feelings by changing some of the activities over which one does have voluntary control. Hence, the advice often given to the depressed person: "Go out and do something, a movie or a game of tennis!"

3. Feelings are nonrepresentational. The representation relation is difficult to characterize. One possibility is to require that, for one thing to represent another, one must be able to identify a systematic mapping between the features ofthe representation and the features of the thing represented. Pain, though caused by an object external to the individual, does not represent the object because the quality of the pain does not vary systematically with featural variation in the object.

4. The identification and description of feeling is based on a subjectively recognized phenomenological quality. One identifies a current feeling to be nausea or nervousness by the *way* it feels. One employs metaphors to describe the quality: "a sinking feeling," "butterflies in the stomach," "a lump in the throat," and so on. Contrast this with the way one identifies a thought or a belief in terms of its intentional content.

5. Feelings differ from one another not only in quality but also in degree. One can be very cold, slightly nauseated, or much more hungry than one was an hour ago. Comparison by degree does not make sense in the case of knowledge, for example.

6. Feelings are mental events occurring within the causal order. It makes sense to talk of feelings being caused by, and causing, something.

A passion, according to Hume, is a simple impression of reflexion. It is certainly possible to read into this picture a naive feeling hypothesis. Passions are elements of conscious experience occurring within the causal order. Hume surmises that, though we are unable to define it, we all know what pride is and recognize it on the basis of introspection. This concurs with the 'quality of experience' feature of feeling. I maintain further that Hume's passions are nonrepresentational. My reading is in contention with the propositional interpretations of Hume's account of pride given by Davidson and Baier.[4] I offer the following in defense of my position: Hume insists that a passion is a *simple*, unanalyzable impression. Were it the case that a passion represented its object, or even its cause, then we would be able to match features of the object (or cause) with features of the emotion. An inverse mapping would uncover the internal structure of a passion—thus contradicting Hume's tenet. Finally, the passions, being caused by an external occurrence—an object's having properties—are not under direct voluntary control.

Descartes claims that the passions "are excitations of the soul which are referred to it in particular and which are caused, maintained and strength- -ened by some movement of the spirits."[5] Since they do not originate in the soul, as do voluntary actions, they are not directly under voluntary control. It is consistent with Descartes' locating the passions in the soul that they are consciously experienced and identifiable by introspection. Given the Cartesian framework of mind-body interaction, the passions are clearly within the causal order. Descartes goes into great detail, tracing the origins of individual passions from external situations through the excitation of the spirits to the excitation of the soul. The passions are distinguished from other perceptions and knowings in that they refer to affectations of the soul and not to an external object or state of the body. This, I believe, marks them as nonrepresentational. But there is a serious difficulty in matching my classification of mental phenomena with that of Descartes's. The points I consider above suggest the conclusion that Descartes's passions are what I conceive to be feelings. The problem is that pain according to Descartes refers to the body, which would give it representational powers. Yet I claim that pain is a feeling and therefore nonrepresentational.

Other considerations lend plausibility to the naive feeling hypothesis. Emotions are introspectable and, according to most, are elements of consciousness. Typical emotions, such as anger, love, and joy, suggest particular feelings. Further, one frequently comes across the linguistic construction "feeling X," where X is an emotion label. One can be very happy, a little

---

[4] See articles by D. Davidson and A. Baier, *op. cit.*

[5] *Passions of the Soul*, First Part, Article 27.

depressed, or not as angry as one was an hour ago. Emotions are not—or at least do not appear to be—under direct voluntary control. Everything turns on the question of the representational characteristic. This is a vindication of Kenny's choosing object directedness to be *the* feature that distinguishes emotion from sensation. I do not wish to enter the debate at this point, though clearly certain views on object directedness automatically preclude the naive feeling hypothesis. Even if one does not press this point, there are other reasons for questioning this hypothesis. One is that the support for the feeling hypothesis offered above fails to provide unique support for it. But even if one accepts all the points mentioned above, conflicting views are not excluded.

The fact that "feels *X*" applies to emotions is not sufficient support for the naive feeling hypothesis. It is safe to assume that the statement "*A* feels *X*" reports that *A* experiences a certain feeling. It does not follow from this that *X* is a feeling. One need only think of cases like "Jake feels betrayed" and "Janet feels guilty" to be convinced of this. I speculate on one possible way of interpreting these sentences. The first reports that the feeling that Jake is currently experiencing is of the type one usually feels when one has been betrayed; the second reports that Janet feels the way one feels when one is guilty. This is what I have called in Chapter 5 a "derivative" use of the predicates. I refrain from further involvement in the question of the semantics of the verb "feel."

A more serious test of a naive feeling hypothesis comes from the consideration of how emotions are individuated. This is a problem for a naive feeling hypothesis because emotions seem to be far more finely differentiated than are qualities of feeling, and the facts one brings to bear in identifying emotions are not limited to the way they feel. Even if one is persuaded that the emotion of anger can be associated with a particular quality of feeling, this is not conclusive evidence for the claim that anger is identical with this feeling. Consider whether one could distinguish, on the basis of quality of feeling alone, anger from indignation, rage, or frustration. Are one's feelings sufficiently finely differentiated to account for the differences among shame, guilt, and embarrassment; fear, dread, and apprehension; revulsion, disgust, and loathing; and between envy and jealousy, regret and remorse? One might achieve some differentiation on the basis of degree alone, as, say, with fear and apprehension or anger and rage. But, clearly, this does not account for all the differences.

Fritjof Bergman brings a similar point to bear on the thesis that emotions are sensations in denying that quality of sensation is the only factor that determines the type of the emotion. The identification is unsound because "if there are so many emotions and the kinds of sensations are fewer, then there cannot be two different sensations for every difference between emotions."[6] He concludes that there is more to emotion than sensation. He offers shame and embarrassment as examples of emotions that are distinguished not by a difference in sensation but on the basis of a judgment. The *ashamed* subject judges that he has performed a morally wrong action. This judgment is partially constitutive of shame. By contrast, embarrassment results when one thinks *others* disapprove of one's actions and is independent of one's own approbation of the action.

Weighing the points in favor of a naive feeling hypothesis and those against it, the final challenge swings the balance against it—especially since none of the points in favor back a *naive* feeling hypothesis exclusively. Many others have responded to the difficult question of how one individuates emotion by taking an emotion to be a complex phenomenon. Wilson suggests a combination of thinking, desiring, and feeling; Mandler and Lazarus suggest a combination of cognition and arousal. In this way, they augment the pool of potential individuating factors. Although the role of feeling in these theories is diminished, it is maintained as an important factor in emotion. Solomon, by contrast, eliminates feeling altogether from his analysis of emotion. He argues that an emotion is a complex array of judgments. Marks, another who deprives emotion of feeling, suggests that feeling is a by-product of emotion.

My position favors the move to greater complexity in the conception of emotion. I am also in favor of preserving a central role for feeling in emotion, finding that Solomon's and Mark's suggestions fly in the face of our most basic intuitions about the nature of emotion—either this, or we are required to revise our conceptions of the cognitive acts they propose as the constituents of emotions. But I do not find it easy to characterize my position as a natural extension of any other that incorporates the two theses. It makes no sense to ask whether an active emotion *is* a feeling or whether a feeling is a part of an active emotion, given the nonepisodic nature of an active emotion. Therefore, I start from scratch, explicating the role of feeling in nonepisodic, relational emotions.

The general framework for feeling episodes in emotional relations is no different from the one described for both action and thought. In the

---

[6] F. Bergman, "A Monologue on the Emotions," in *Understanding Human Emotions*, p. 18.

patterns of events referred to by most emotion terms, there are events in which the subject experiences feelings. Further, some of the conditionals implied by the emotion constrain the occurrences of these feeling episodes. I draw answers to some of the difficult questions raised above from this general picture. In particular, I offer a way to deal with the recurring question of what feelings have to do with the identification of an emotion. I sidestep certain other problematic questions—for example, the question of whether the feeling associated with emotion is a special emotional feeling or is a generic state of arousal or depression. I decide certain questions by assumption. I assume, for example, that there are differentiated feeling states that are relevant to emotions where differentiation is not sufficiently fine grain to account for the variation in all types of emotion.

As suggested above, the pattern of an emotional relation includes events in which the subject experiences the appropriate feelings. The type of the emotional relation is determined by two features of the feeling episodes. First, certain types of emotions are associated with certain qualities of feeling. Second, the emotion type is associated with a systematic correlation between the quality of feeling and context of arousal. The second factor, which is none other than the constraints imposed on feeling episodes, is a key to the solution of many of the persistent problems raised above. It in effect gives my account an extra variable. Before I show the application of my theory to several examples, I describe one further theoretical principle.

Individuation of emotion was the downfall of the naive feeling hypothesis. To get around this obstacle, theorists moved toward a picture of a more complex and variegated emotion. The move to greater complexity is not sufficient to get around the problem *if* one continues to maintain that there is a signature feeling to each emotion, much like the serial number on a motored appliance. This would be subject to the same criticisms as the naive feeling hypothesis was. The two views make the same problematic assumption: that there is a one-to-one connection between the type of the emotion and the type of the feeling. There are two ways the assumption may be weakened; only one of them is demanded by the nature of the problem. There are too few feelings to go around. Therefore, there must be distinct emotions with common feeling constituents. The advantage of the constraints associated with instances of emotion becomes evident here. Distinct emotions in which feeling episodes are qualitatively identical are distinguished by the uniqueness of the contexts of arousal of the feelings. This is the weakening of a naive feeling hypothesis that the solution to the problem requires. But a further move is possible: There may be more than one quality of feeling associated with a single emotion type. Both weakenings of the one-to-one connection occur.

Perhaps a few examples would elucidate the main points. With the examples, I leave the domain of the active emotions momentarily. Shame and embarrassment form a pair of distinct emotions with a common feeling element. My position suggests that the type of an emotion determines the quality of the feelings involved in it. The pair shows us that the determination is not unique. In these sorts of cases, the constraints make all the difference. The feeling of shame-embarrassment in the case of embarrassment is aroused when one thinks that *others* are critical of one's actions or state of appearance. One enters a room in which a party is being held. The people in a group standing nearby begin to stare and giggle. One experiences a feeling of shame-embarrassment. In the case of shame the feeling is aroused when one recognizes one's own wrongdoing or state of appearance. Experiencing shame-embarrassment when one realizes one has behaved in a morally reprehensible way satisfies one of the constraints of shame. In other words, shame and embarrassment differ in having the feeling aroused, systematically, in different types of contexts.

Let us return to the case of Julia's envy. In applying the term envy to the relation between Julia and Pamela, one intends it to cover several feeling episodes. These include Julia's feeling agitated, bitter, smug, and pleased. They are part of the envy pattern and satisfy several constraints. Julia feels bitter when Pamela is awarded the prize for "Most Valuable Novice." She is agitated when she thinks about the possibility of losing a really important case to Pamela, feels smug when Pamela's proposal is voted down at a meeting, and feels pleased when another colleague berates Pamela's performance on a case. Daniel's loving his father includes Daniel's feeling a surge of warmth on seeing his father after a long separation, anxiety when he hears of his father's ill health, fury on hearing how his father was cheated by the insurance company, and pleased when his father praises him.

We see now why the question of whether there is one feeling per emotion or a generic state of arousal that is common to all is a spurious one. Quality of feeling is an important factor, but it does not tell the whole story about the emotion. One considers the contexts of arousal of the subject's feelings—that is, the conditions that the occurrence of a feeling episode satisfies. The constraining features include external environmental factors, features of the subject's mental state, and the subject's activities at the time. This affects the way one interprets the phrases "feels love," "feels envy," and "feels fear." They describe an individual's feeling state; but that is not all. The descriptions apply to the individual's state not only by virtue of the quality of the individual's current experience but also by virtue of the context of its arousal and its presence within a certain pattern of episodes. It is helpful to recall the parallel but simpler example given in Chapter 5 of David preparing for a dinner party. One describes David's activity of laying silverware on the table with the expression "preparing for a dinner party" only if David *is* preparing for a dinner party and this activity is part of the pattern. If not, the activity might be described "cleaning the silverware," "stealing the silverware," or simply "laying the silverware on the table."

I consider feeling to be an extremely important aspect of emotion, although I give it no special place within my theoretical framework. Feeling episodes have their places in emotional relations alongside actions and thinking. A more detailed development of the theory might account for feeling's prominent role in emotion. Possibly feelings occur more frequently than other emotionally relevant episodes. Or feelings might be considered an essential ingredient to any pattern that is conceived to be an emotion. This would explain why feeling has epistemic prominence in the identification of emotion. Feeling provides an excellent clue in detecting the presence of an emotion. A feeling episode frequently signals an emotional relation. One might not apply the term "love" to a relationship until one experiences the feeling of longing when the loved one leaves. Similarly in the parallel drawn to the case of Dobbs preparing to murder: One views his activities as at most eccentric until the buying of the knife clues one to his possible intent to murder. The other events are reorganized accordingly, in retrospect.

The possibilities for variation among different types of emotional relations are vast. Certain emotions might involve a greater number of feeling episodes than others. 'Intellectual' emotions, as have been cited in the appreciation of art, might indeed involve little feeling. Emotions vary in the range of qualities of feeling they involve. A love relation is frequently rich in its variety of feeling. Fear is more limited. I have all along acknowledged the existence of episodic emotions as well as nonepisodic. Certain episodic emotions are associated with very specific qualities of feeling. I number among these rage, fury, and elation. This dimension probably interacts with another, which is the extent to which the emotional relation infiltrates aspects of one's life. Some, like love, weave into a significant portion of a person's life. Thoughts, actions, and feelings associated with the loved individual are conditioned upon a wide spectrum of factors that the person encounters. Fear is more easily compartmentalized. In fearing the neighbor's dog, the actions, thoughts and feelings, covered by the relation are restricted within well-defined boundaries—namely, within a certain distance of the dog. If these sorts of fears spill over excessively into the aspects of a person's life, we judge it pathological and label the individual's state "paranoia" or "obsession."

4. Salience

We notice, attend to, and remember only a fraction of the information that is available to us in a given situation. It is assumed that the salience of selected features in certain situations is not a random phenomenon. For example, almost everyone notices when their names are spoken even with considerable background noise. Many rules have been proposed to account for the systematic salience of certain types of factors to certain individuals. These range from commonsense accusations such as "You don't hear what it does not suit you to hear!" to the complex laws governing Freud's notion of repression or selective memory. Motives and goals influence what a person apprehends, thinks about, and remembers. Emotions do, too. These factors are responsible for vast individual differences. I recall vividly an incident in high school in which a teacher made a public fool of me. A classmate, having experienced the incident from a different perspective, barely remembers it. There are innumerable examples from real life. In this section, I examine some of the connections that are posited between an emotion and the salience of certain types of phenomena. I show that the conception of an emotional relation provides a natural framework within which to explicate the connection between emotion and salience.

Consider the following examples of the way an emotion is tied to the salience of selected features of the environment. Recall the case of Martin's fearing his neighbor's bullmastiff. Martin is sure to be sensitive to information about the dog's proximity. Since he is on the 'lookout' for it, he is more likely to notice the dog than someone who is emotionally neutral to it. His awareness of the dog is matched only, paradoxically, by the monster's doting owner. Julia's envying Pamela involves a similar focusing of her attention. Out of the hum and chatter of cafeteria noises, she manages to eavesdrop on the firm's partners' conversation about Pamela's handling of a case. She is watchful of subtle cues reflecting the attitudes of colleagues to Pamela, measuring them against their attitudes to her. Julia easily recalls the incidents that confirm her grounds for envy and thinks about Pamela and Pamela's status in the firm in a way that might be termed "obsessive." Few remember the despicable acts of an individual more readily than the one who despises him. These examples display what I shall call *the attention-directing quality of emotion.*

Hume claims that thinking about an individual's admirable qualities causes the passion of love. The virtuous individual is the object of love. The attention-directing quality of emotion suggests an alternative order of things. One notices the person's virtues *because* one loves the person and not vice versa, as Hume suggests. Reid puts the point succinctly:

> It (the passion) gives often a strange bias to the judgement, making a man quicksighted in everything that tends to inflame his passion, and to justify it, but blind to everything that tends to moderate and allay it.[7]

This raises a question: Which comes first, the perception of virtue or love? I think that one need not be forced into affirming either, exclusively. My view defuses the issue somewhat because it denies that emotions are episodic and therefore the question of which causes which is not easily interpretable.

Sartre calls emotion a "magical transformation of the world."[8] Taken at face value this remark is obscure and suggests a touch of the mystical. However, we may take Sartre's remark to be a more dramatic way of pointing to emotion's attention-directing quality. Because one attends selectively to one's surroundings, two individuals in the same situation might notice distinct configurations of features. They see the situation in distinct ways. In a manner of speaking, they see distinct situations. Emotions systematically affect the way one's attention is drawn toward, and away from, certain types of phenomena. They transform the world by drastically affecting one's perspective. Imagine a situation in which three individuals A, B, and C are attending a dinner party. They each bear a distinct emotional relation to the guest of honor. A admires the guest, B detests him, and C is emotionally neutral to him. The next day, A is eager to talk about the guest's wit, charm, and quiet reserve; B remembers the guest's constant interruptions, his egocentric stories, and his snobbish attitude toward other guests; C remembers very little except the man's remarkable red hair. The

---

[7]   T. Reid, *Essays on the Active Powers of the Human Mind*, p. 176.

[8]   J. P. Sartre, *The Emotions: Outline of Theory*, p. 59.

diverse emotional relations have 'transformed' the man in the eyes of each of the guests in that each perceives him to have a distinct set of properties.

Up till now, I have run together two distinct though related phenomena under the heading "salience." They share the idea that in ascertaining what things are salient to a given individual one gains insight into the individual's styles or habits of thought or of apprehending a situation. In the first case, the salience of a phenomenon is reflected in the sheer frequency of thinking about it, and in the concentration of these thoughts. In being in love, one thinks frequently of the other person and daydreams and fantasizes about situations in which one is in the company of that person. One spontaneously recalls pleasant meetings with the person. One might make this notion more precise by describing it in terms of the "likelihood of thinking about a given phenomenon." A phenomenon is salient over a certain period if the likelihood of thinking about it is greater than some average.

In the second case, salience is viewed as a relation between what exists in an individual's environment and what the individual apprehends. Certain features or objects are salient to an individual if it is the case that if these are present to the subject, either directly perceivable or indirectly referred to through another medium, the individual notices the features or objects. Pamela is salient to Julia in their working environment in that Julia attends closely to any information about Pamela that might be present. This covers what is directly in her visual field, what she hears others say, or what she infers from facts that bear a more subtle relation to Pamela. His neighbor's bullmastiff is also salient to Martin in this sense. Actually, one should be more precise in describing the salience of certain phenomena. The bullmastiff is salient to Martin only as far as its possible presence nearby is concerned. He is not likely to take interest in the dog's excellent pedigree, though he is likely to focus on information about the dog's ill health. The salience of the guest of honor to the three guests is similarly subject to qualification. His virtues are particularly salient to A and his vices to B; C shows no systematic pattern in the way he focusses attention on the guest.

Emotional Relations and Salience.   It is a direct consequence of my conception of an emotional relation that certain objects and features are salient to an emotion's subject. This is a substantial departure from the picture that an emotion *causes* a change in the subject's pattern of attention. According to my theory, the fact that certain phenomena are salient to a certain individual partially *constitutes* the fact that the individual is emotionally related to the phenomenon. The two types of salience correspond to the two paradigms of analysis of emotional relations, restricted to thinking. First, the changes in frequency and concentration of certain types of thoughts marking the salience of a phenomenon is precisely one of the factors that mark an emotion pattern. The emotion does not *cause* the salience of certain phenomena; their salience in part *constitutes* the emotion. Salience of certain phenomena as featured in the second conception can be described by statements of the following type: If an individual is in a situation of type *A*, she apprehends *B*. This corresponds to the second aspect of emotional relatedness: its constraining function on the subject's interactions with the emotion's focus. One describes an individual's selective attention to a particular type of phenomenon as the "salience" of the phenomenon to the individual. But salience in this sense coincides with the constraining function of an emotional relation on the interactions between the subject and the emotion's focus. In other words, an event that illustrates the salience of a given object to an individual might easily instantiate an emotional relation with the object. This follows from the fact that many of the constraints implied by an emotional relation condition the occurrence of a cognitive response on the presence of certain selected features of the surroundings.

5. Summary

In this chapter, I elaborate my picture of emotion. In Chapter 5, I argued that an emotion is an abstraction over a sequence of events and a number of constraints. In applying an emotion concept to an individual, one picks out the structured interaction between the individual and an item in the world. This structured interaction is characterized not only in terms of the types of events of which it is constituted, but by the nature of the pattern of occurrence that these events follow. This is the reason for using the term *pattern of events* and not *collection of events*. The events out of which an emotion is built fit certain specifications. It is not the case that *any* old event is the possible constituent of an emotion pattern. I suggested three categories of events that contribute to the making of an emotion: thought, action, and feeling. More precisely, the events involve the subject of the emotion in thinking, acting, and feeling. I suggested possible scenarios for emotional relations, matching certain types of emotions with certain types of thoughts, actions, and feelings. I discussed salience because it is a phenomenon that is frequently associated with emotion and is easily accommodated within my new framework. I analyzed salience in terms of an emergent property of a number of events in which the subject is thinking or apprehending something. This is shown to correspond to the part of an emotion pattern to which thought-events contribute.

In the concluding chapter, I circle back to the question of object directedness, showing how my analysis of emotion and emotional relatedness yields an analysis of the relation of emotion to focus.

PART THREE

Emotion and Focus

Chapter 7

Emotion and Focus

I began this work by drawing attention in Part One to the importance of object directedness in the conception of emotion. I argued that there is a need to resolve the confusion that abounds in connection with the objects of emotion. Part Two grew out of the premise that an accurate conception of emotion contributes to the understanding of object directedness. I now reconnect these two halves of my work. The discussion in Part One led to a reappraisal of the concept of object directedness and to the conclusion that the notion be dissolved into its conceptual subunits. In Part Two, I examined and offered an analysis of the class of active emotions. These emotions are not episodic properties of individuals but dispositional relations between the emotion's subject and another individual or nonhuman part of the world. In this final chapter, I explicate the connection between the new conception of active emotions and the analysis of one of the conceptual subunits of object directedness: relation to a focus.

I conclude the chapter with a brief look at directions for future research that are suggested by my conception of emotion and emotion's directedness.

1. Relation to a Focus

The gist of my proposed resolution, in bringing to bear the conception of emotional relatedness on the question of object directedness, is this: Others take the statement "Frank loves Susan" to be a description of Frank's love, which has Susan as its object. It has proved problematic to analyze the relation between Frank and Susan by virtue of which Susan is the object of Frank's love. My proposal is that love is itself relational. The statement therefore describes a love relation between Frank and Susan. There is no longer any need to introduce the notion of object directedness into the picture.

If this were the only contribution of my analysis of active emotional relations to the understanding of emotion's object directedness, one would justifiably be disappointed in it. For, clearly, it explains very little. First, one may question the apparently ad hoc decision to conceive of emotions relationally. The arguments of Chapter 4 had direct bearing only on the thesis that emotions are universally occurrent. I have yet to give independent backing to the claim that certain emotions are relations. Second, the gloss is unsatisfying because it offers no insight into the workings of the relation that I refer to with the rather mystifying expression "emotional relation." Below, I meet these skeptical challenges without making substantial additions to the content of the preceding chapters. I account for the active emotions' relational nature and expose the workings of the relations themselves.

Recall some of the examples of emotions to which the new theory is relevant:

1. Frank loves Susan.
2. Meryl loathes her boss.
3. Martin fears his neighbor's bullmastiff.
4. Phoebe fears the campus rapist.
5. Paul regrets having refused to invest in Apple Computers.
6. Julia envies Pamela.
7. Lynne is angry at Dennis.
8. Lynne is angry at the person who dented her car.

I include sentences 7 and 8 for illustrative purposes. Though anger does not fit the specifications for active emotions, it is similar to the active emotions in not satisfying the two theses discussed in Chapter 4. What does the analysis of emotional relatedness tell us about these statements and, in particular, about 1?

The statement "Frank loves Susan" applies at the level of individual events to a sequence of varied but conceptually linked events. The events, generally construed, are of three types—ones in which the subject is thinking, acting, or feeling. Of course, some events might involve combinations of these activities—the subject both thinking and acting, for example. The emotional relation is identified to be of the type 'love' by virtue of the nature of the subject's thinking, acting, and feeling. Frank thinks often about Susan. He marvels at her perceptiveness and sense of humor. He experiences a thrill of delight on seeing her after a long separation. He enjoys spending time with her. He arranges lavish birthday parties for her. The love relation suggests certain dispositions. Frank becomes annoyed on hearing Susan insulted by one of his colleagues. In passing the local pub, he recalls the events leading to their first meeting. If Susan criticizes something he has done, it causes him to experience a feeling of displeasure. If, at a social gathering, Susan pays much attention to any other man, Frank feels jealous and tries to intervene. If Susan is needful of anything, Frank gallantly sets out to meet the need. Events and constraints of this type are not constitutive of every love relation. In a different setting and with different individuals, the events and dispositions might take on an entirely different shape, as long as they remain within the limits of the conception of love. No matter what the context, the concept might preclude that a love relation involve the subject voluntarily hurting the one she loves against that individual's will.

Aside from the types of the events, the conditions they satisfy, and their patterns of occurrence, there is an additional factor that I have not stressed sufficiently that is definitive of the love relation between Frank and Susan. It is the roles played by Frank and Susan. In each of the events determined a constituent of the love relation, Frank features as the subject of thinking, feeling, or acting. Susan fills a complementary role consistently throughout the events. Frank thinks about *Susan* and it is on account of *Susan* that Frank feels happy, sad, annoyed, and jealous. Frank's role as an agent occurs in situations in which Susan plays a significant part, either in initiating the action or in being its object. This is the rationale behind my conception of emotional relatedness. *The emotion is a relation because it is an abstraction over a pattern of events that are themselves relational.* In the example above, Frank's and Susan's being related by love is derivative of a sequence of events. Each event in the sequence displays an aspect of the structured interaction between Frank and Susan. Frank is the lover and Susan the loved one by virtue of the roles they take consistently throughout the sequence of episodes. The individuals Frank and Susan are common threads in the train of events covered by the love relation.

I leave the domain of emotion to explicate further the idea of a sequence of events that are unified because of the way their roles are filled. Consider the work of a biographer. Her goal is to accumulate and record as much information about her subject, Archibald Smith, as possible. Let us say the information covers Smith's place and date of birth, his familial origins, his childhood experiences, his education, his marriages, his deeds of great moment, and the details of his fascinating social life. To the entire collection of events one applies the label "The Life of Archibald Smith." The events covered by the label have one very important thing in common— they involve Archibald Smith. In the case of a person's life history, this might be the only common factor.

Consider the enormous array of events constituting the life of Archibald Smith. One can see that the array of events defines a role—the role that is actually played by A. Smith. A *role* is defined in the set of events in the following way. Instead of talking about Archibald, I begin the story by mentioning that there exists an individual who was born in 1925. The rest of the story follows an iterative pattern: The person who was born in 1925 came from a working-class family. The person who was born in 1925 and came from a working-class family was fluent in three languages by the age of seven. And so on. The role is an abstract phenomenon that emerges from the sequence of events. In placing actual individuals in the events, roles must be preserved. It must be Archibald Smith who was born in 1925, was born to a working-class family, and who could speak three languages fluently by the time he was seven years old. The same types of events, with distinct subjects, no longer constitute "The Life of Archibald Smith."[2]

Here is another description of a set of occurrences. I omit the the names of its individual protagonists to further clarify my point: (The *s are not variables. They signify *gaps*, that is, places for names or variables.)

- Since Christmas, * has spent every weekend with *.
- * bought * an expensive wristwatch on the 14th of February.
- * states repeatedly that * is attractive, talented, kind, and wonderful company.
- * saw * dancing with * and felt insanely jealous.
- * became furious when * was overlooked for promotion.
- Frequently, when * is alone, * thinks about *.
- If * sees a threat to *, * does everything possible to avert it.
- * tries to comply with *'s every request.

---

[2] J. Barwise and J. Perry give a precise definition of a role in their metaphysics of situations. I attempt to use this notion here but outside the context of their theory. Whether or not my loose description of a role is capable of being sharpened to fit exactly with theirs is not important. I merely use it as a tool to *explicate*, and not to construct, my notion of emotional relatedness.

- Being in *'s company gives * a warm glow of contentment and a faith in the meaningfulness of life.
- And so forth.

With no information about how individuals are assigned to the *s, there is no reason to see the statements as about anything but a collection of diverse events. However, from the complex description, I could derive roles by requiring that the *s in the positions 1, 3, 5, 7, 10, 11, 12, 14, 16, 17, and 19 be substituted by the name of a single individual and all the others, aside from position 9, by the name of one other. If one is willing to forgo misgivings about the caricatured portrayal of love, one might see that the statements describe a love relation. It is a love relation because two conditions are met: First, the types of events described fit the conception of love according to their pattern of occurrence and instantiation of certain conditionals (given the appropriate contextual background) and, second, the roles defined above correspond to those that would be required of a love relation. The love relation holds between two individuals only, despite the presence of the third individual. Minor characters who do not persist throughout the sequence of events do not earn a place in the emotional relation. The slimy Etienne, playing the part defined by position 9, who is constantly vying for Susan's attentions takes no part in the love relation between Frank and Susan.

What I have said about a love relation can be extended to cover other types of emotions including ones that involve relations to other *types* of relata. The picture to fix in one's mind is the picture of an array of events conceptually identified by the type of the emotion and tied together further by the persistence of at least two items: the subject of the emotion and another individual (or possibly other items). Given the emotional relation L, the individuals F and S, and setting s,

$L(F, S)$, if and only if, F and S fill the appropriate roles
  defined by L for F and S in s.

In other words, F and S stand in the emotional relation L if and only if they feature appropriately in a sequence of events that reflect the pattern and satisfy the constraints prescribed by the type of L and the features of the context of L.

Most emotional relations are not commutative. Therefore, it matters which individual fills which role in the string of episodes. If Frank loves Susan, then Frank fills the subject role throughout the sequence of episodes and Susan fills the role of love's focus. The subject of an emotion is so called because she systematically takes the role of subject in the episodes that constitute an emotional relation. She is the agent, the one who is thinking, and the one who is feeling. In every emotional relation there is a subject role filled by the subject of the emotion. The label "focus of emotion" applies to any other individual who features throughout the pattern of episodes and in the constraints on the episodes. In the case of a two-place emotional relation there is one other individual who features in every emotional episode and is the emotion's focus.

There is an important difference between the conceptions of an emotion related to an object and an emotion related to a focus. In the first case one pictures an individual undergoing a certain experience that is recognized to be an emotion. The subject is experiencing envy, hatred, resentment, or loathing, for example. These emotions are directed to objects. An assumption that grounds the search for an analysis of the emotion-object relation, is that there exists one type of relation holding between the subject's hatred and its object, the subject's resentment and its object, the subject's envy and its object, and the subject's loathing and its object. This is the relation that Wilson, Hume, Kenny, and the others try to analyze. According to my picture, all that is common to instances of envy, hatred, resentment, and loathing is the fact that they are emotional relations. But they are distinct relations. This is comparable to the cases "to the left of," "above," "next to," and "two miles away from," which are all spatial relations, but distinct ones. In applying the label "focus" to one of the relata, I do not suggest that there is a real element of focusing in each of these emotions. It stems from the formal character of the analysis. The focus is a fixed point around which the events constituting the emotions revolve. Properly speaking, the subject is also a focus of the emotion because it is a fixed point throughout the pattern. I keep the label "subject" because of the asymmetry that demands that the subject and focus be distinguished according to the different roles they play in an emotional relation.

Up to now, I have allowed an imprecise use of the term "focus." One finds in the literature on object directedness that the terms "object of emotion" and "focus of emotion" are used interchangeably. The former is much more common. I have followed this tendency, but because of the noted differences between my new technical notion of an emotion's focus I recommend that we reserve the use of this label for the cases in which the technical notion is applicable.

The case of Julia's envy illustrates a three-place emotional relation. This raises a problem for an analysis of the emotion-object relation. Which is the object of Julia's envy, Pamela or Pamela's superior job status? My view treats envy like any other three-place relation. Like the relation described in "X buying Y from Z," Julia's envy can have two foci each of which has its unique role in the pattern and constraints of the envy relation.

2. Intentionality

I claim to have analyzed an aspect of object directedness, relation to a focus. I do not, however, claim to have analyzed the intentionality out of emotion. An emotional relation holds between two individuals if and only if their interactions fit a certain pattern and instantiate certain conditionals. Situations in which the subject is thinking about the other individual are numbered among those that are relevant to the emotion. I assume that it makes sense to posit a relation between two individuals A and B consisting in A's thinking about B. I take A thinking that B is cruel and A wondering how to make B's life unpleasant to be situations in which A and B are related by virtue of A's intentional mental state. I offer no suggestions for analyzing *this* relation. Although I maintain that the case described in "Hannah is angry that she was not invited to the party" is partially relational, there is an aspect that remains unanalyzed until one develops a theory of intentionality for emotional states. This follows from the the idea that Hannah's state of anger, as it is described above, represents the information that she was not invited to the party. My analyses of the active emotions and relatedness to a focus has no bearing on how to account for the representational capacity of these types of cases.

Although my analysis is aimed at a strictly relational aspect of emotion, it sheds light on one type of case that is persistently brought to light as a counterexample to a relational view of directedness. Philosophers have used this type of case to ground their dissatisfaction with a relational view of emotion's directedness. I speak of cases in which the emotion is directed but for which no real relatum exists. Imagine the case of Kristin, who believes that her friend was murdered and hates the man who murdered her. In fact, Kristin's friend committed suicide, so there is no man who fits the description.

The case does not pose a problem for my analysis because I deny that Kristin's emotion has a focus. In examining any full-blown case of an emotional relation, it is possible to isolate the subject and to ignore anything going on outside her. Usually, "Frank is embracing Susan" describes a relation between Frank and Susan. If one chooses to ignore the relational information, one perceives only an activity performed by Frank. Take a case of hatred that is identical in type to Kristin's hatred in all ways but one—in this case the murderer exists. On the basis of features of the subjects alone, Kristin's hatred may be indistinguishable from the hatred of the second subject.[3] One continues to see Kristin's state as "directed" hatred because its subjective features strongly resemble those of a genuine case of hatred; but it is only half the picture. Even though on the basis of subjective features we continue to apply the term "hatred" to the situation involving Kristin, it is not a bona fide case of hatred because it is not relational. Ultimately, whether "Kristin hates her friend's murderer" is judged an appropriate description of the situation is a separate question for a semantics of emotion sentences to decide.

3. Summary and Conclusion

Hume's picture of emotion as a simple experiential phenomenon has given way to more complicated characterizations. I add a new dimension by suggesting that an emotion is a pattern that is comprised of a number of distinct occurrences. Even though emotions are stretched out, nonuniform phenomena, they are attributed sufficient structure to account for many of the features we typically associate with emotions. Emotions involve thought, feeling, and action; my picture accounts for this. One type of emotion can take many different forms, depending on the subject and the context of its occurrence. This, too, is accounted for by the fact that the pattern is determined by the type of the emotion, features of the subject and of other central participants, and the nature of the context. The dispositional nature of emotion consists in the systematic connection of certain of the events in the pattern with certain others, and the cooccurrence of certain phenomena within the events that comprise the pattern. Salience of certain individuals and properties, so often associated with emotion, is easily placed within the pattern.

Even object directedness, the elusive and troublesome feature, finds resolution within the new framework. In accounting for object directedness

---

[3] On the other hand, because action directed to the focus is a constituent of most emotional relations, Kristin's hatred (and that of the second subject) has a limited range. So, even if one limits one's vision to the subjective element, Kristin's hatred lacks certain crucial elements.

I make two important qualifications of scope. The analysis of Part One warns of the futility of seeking a global analysis of the concept of object directedness. I select one of its aspects—relation to a focus. Second, I choose to look only at the class of what I call "active emotions." An emotion pattern involves a further crucial uniformity: a number of individuals (and, possibly, items in the world) that feature in each event that fits it. These individuals are *related* by the emotion. The one is the subject of the emotion; the other (or others), the emotion's focus.

Looking at the complex, though structured, sequence of events that comprises an emotional relation, one realizes the power and convenience of the simple statements with which we began: Frank loves Susan, Meryl loathes her boss, Julia envies Pamela. Emotion concepts cover complex, structured interactions between their subjects and real parts of the subjects' environment.

4. Directions for Future Research

I propose substantial changes to standardly held positions on emotion and emotion's object directedness: first, in suggesting that there no longer is a place for the notion of object directedness in the conception of emotion and, second, in providing a new set of individuative principles for a significant subset of emotions. According to the principles, these emotions are nonoccurrent and relational. My work is mainly devoted to establishing a new framework for the study of emotion. I manage to develop some of the ideas, but only within a limited domain. I would like to expand the domain for example, by including noncpisodic cmotions that arc not active. Anger, which figures prominently in the writings of psychologists, falls within this domain. I see the need, too, for a more detailed study of individual emotions. I believe that my work also has significant implications for a semantics of emotion sentences.

Aspects of emotional episodes take the place of emotion's objects. I limit my examination of these aspects to one: the emotion's focus. Although this covers cases such as A loves B, C is angry at D, and E is worried about F's health, there are significant omissions. In particular, the cases in which the subject's state is considered to have a representational relation to an objective event are least understood. This includes cases like "Hannah is angry that she was not invited to the party." Questions about the other aspects—explanatory factors, or relations to properties—are worth pursuing. To cover the ground previously covered by the unsuccessful notion of object directedness, all the aspects need to be systematically examined. The advantage of the plurality of aspects is that it gives the freedom to theorize about each concept independently of the others.

In explicating my theory of the active emotions, I noted the need for a more detailed look at the constituents of emotional relations and how they enter into various types of emotions. We would need to look deeply into single emotion types and consider the interactions among the conceptual and contextual factors. With knowledge of the more subtle aspects of emotional relations, my theory has the potential to give insight into questions about the difference, for example, between anger and indignation, between despising and hating and between loving and admiring. The far-reaching goal is to carry this new notion of nonepisodic emotion into the empirical realm.

Appendix

A   (emotion verb) *B*
A: proper name, pronoun, definite description
B: noun phrase

Emotion Verb: abhors, admires, adores, approves (of), despises, detests, dreads, enjoys, envies, fears, hates, likes, loves, regrets, resents, respects, worries (about, that).

A   *is* (emotion) *B*
A: proper name, pronoun, definite description
B: prepositional clause, *that*-clause, prepositional phrase

Emotion (preposition, *that*): afraid (of, that), alarmed (by), amazed (by), angry (that, about, at, with), annoyed (that, over, by), anxious (about, over), appalled (by), apprehensive (about, over), ashamed (of, about), delighted (that, about), depressed (about), disgusted (with, by), distraught (over), distressed (that, by, about), embarrassed (about, over), envious (of), frightened (of), furious (about, that, with), happy (that, about, to), horrified (that, by), incensed (over), indignant (over, about), jealous (of), miserable (about, over), pleased (with, that, to, about, for), proud (of, to , that), remorseful (of), sad (that, about, to), surprised (that, by), terrified (that, to, by), troubled (by, over), vexed (that, by), worried (that, by).

A   *is/feels* (emotion)
A: proper name, pronoun, definite description

Emotion: afraid, alarmed, amazed, amused, angry, annoyed, anxious, appalled, apprehensive, ashamed, delighted, depressed, disappointed, displeased, distraught, distressed, elated, embarrassed, enraptured, envious, frustrated, happy, miserable, jealous, petrified, piqued, pleased, sad, scared, surprised, terrified, vexed, worried.

Bibliographical References

Arnold, M. B., *Emotion and Personality* (2 vols.), Columbia University Press, New York, 1960.

Arnold, M. B., "Human Emotion and Action," in T. Mischel (ed.), *Human Action: Conceptual and Empirical Issues.*

Baier, A., "Hume's Analysis of Pride," *Journal of Philosophy*, vol. LXXV, No. 1, 1978, 27–40.

Barwise, J., and J. Perry, *Situations and Attitudes*, Bradford Books, M.I.T. Press, 1983.

Bedford, E., "Emotions," *Proceedings of the Aristotelian Society, supplement*, vol. 31, 1957.

Bergman, F., "A Monologue on the Emotions," in Bowling Green Studies in Applied Philosophy, *Understanding Human Emotions.*

Blum, L. A., *Friendship, Altruism, and Morality*, Routledge & Kegan Paul, London, Boston, 1980.

Bowling Green Studies in Applied Philosophy, *Understanding Human Emotions*, vol. 1, F. D. Miller, Jr., and T. W. Attig (eds.), Bowling Green, 1979.

Davidson, D., "Hume's Cognitive Theory of Pride," *Journal of Philosophy*, vol. LXXXIII, No. 19, 1976, 744–757.

Davidson, D., "On Saying That," *Synthese*, vol. 19, 1968–69, 130–146.

Descartes, R., *Passions of the Soul*, S. H. Voss (transl.), unpublished manuscript.

Greenspan, P. S., "A Case of Mixed Feelings: Ambivalence and the Logic of Emotion," in A. O. Rorty, *Explaining Emotions.*

Hampshire, S. (ed.), *Philosophy of Mind*, Harper & Row, New York, 1966.

Hume, D., *A Treatise of Human Nature*, L. A. Selby-Bigge (ed.), Oxford University Press, Oxford, 1968 (orig. publ. Oxford, 1888).

Izard, C., *Human Emotions*, Plenum Press, New York, 1977.

James, W., *The Principles of Psychology* (2 vols.), Henry Holt, New York, 1890.

Kenny, A., *Action, Emotion and Will*, Routledge & Kegan Paul, London, 1963.

Lazarus, R. S., A. D. Kanner, and S. Folkman, "Emotion: A Cognitive-Phenomenological Analysis," in R. Plutchik and H. Kellerman, *Emotion: Theory, Research and Experience*, vol. 1.

Leventhal, H., "Toward a Comprehensive Theory of Emotion," in *Advances in Experimental Social Psychology*, vol. 13, Academic Press, New York, 1980.

Marks, J., "A Theory of Emotion," *Philosophical Studies*, vol. 42, 1982, 227–242.

Martin, C. D., and M. Deutcher, "Remembering," *Philosophical Review*, vol. 75, 1966, 161–196.

Mischel, T. (ed.), *Human Action: Conceptual and Empirical Issues*, Academic Press, New York, London, 1969.

Neu, J., "Jealous Thoughts," in A. O. Rorty, *Explaining Emotions*.

Peters, R. S., and C. A. Mace, "Emotions and the Category of Passivity," *Proceedings of the Aristotelian Society*, vol. 62, 1961–62, 111–142.

Plutchik, R., and H. Kellerman, *Emotion: Theory, Research, and Experience*, vol. 1., Academic Press, New York, 1980.

Quine, W. V. O., *Word and Object*, M.I.T. Press, Cambridge, 1960.

Reid, T., *Essays on the Active Powers of the Human Mind*, [Reproduced from Volumes III and IV of *The Works of Thomas Reid*, Samuel Etheridge, Jr., Charlestown, 1813 (vol. I), 1814 (vol. II), 1815 (vol. III, IV)], M.I.T. Press, Cambridge, 1969.

Rorty, A. O., "Explaining Emotions," in A. O. Rorty, *Explaining Emotions*.

Rorty, A. O., *Explaining Emotions*, University of California Press, Berkeley, 1980.

Ryle, G., *The Concept of Mind*, Hutchinson & Co., London, 1949.

Sartre, J., *The Emotions: Outline of a Theory*, Philosophical Library, New York, 1948.

Schachter, S. and J. Singer, "Cognitive, Social and Physiological Determinants of Emotional States," *Psychological Review*, Vol. LXIX, 1962, 379–399.

Solomon, R. C., "Emotion and Choice," in A. O. Rorty, *Explaining Emotions*.

Solomon, R. C., "Nothing to Be Proud of," in Bowling Green Studies in Applied Philosophy, *Understanding Human Emotions*.

Solomon, R. C., *The Passions*, Anchor Press/Doubleday, New York, 1976.

Thalberg, I., "Constituents and Causes of Emotion and Action," *The Philosophical Quarterly*, vol. 23, No. 90, 1973, 1–14.

Thalberg, I., "Emotion and Thought," in S. Hampshire (ed.), *Philosophy of Mind*.

Wade, M. L., *Passion and Volition in Hume's* Treatise, Ph.D. Dissertation, Stanford University, 1982.

Wilson, J. R. S., *Emotion and Object*, Cambridge University Press, Cambridge, 1972.

Wittgenstein, L.,*Philosophical Investigations*,G. E. M. Anscombe(transl.), Basil Blackwell, Oxford (2nd ed.), 1968.

Zajonc, R. B., "Feeling and Thinking: Preferences Need No Inferences," *American Psychologist*, Vol. 35, No. 2, 151–175.